'Drawing on research and personal experience, th
for women who want to return to higher educatic
this with family life. It provides practical strategies for success and also
shows how such women bring tremendous reserves of knowledge and
experience with them, making an invaluable contribution to the learning
environments of universities and colleges.'

Jocey Quinn, Professor of Education, Plymouth Institute of Education

'This short yet rich book is easily accessible and avoids jargon. The
inspirational voices of the case studies illuminate the power of education
to transform learners' lives and their communities.'

Dr Vicky Duckworth, Reader in Education, Edge Hill University

Learn Innovate Aspire

Weston College Group

Tel: 01934 411493   **Email:** library@weston.ac.uk

TXT 2 RENEW: 07860 023339

Juggling Higher Education Study and Family Life

Louise Webber

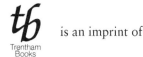 is an imprint of

First published in 2017 by the UCL Institute of Education Press, University College London, 20 Bedford Way, London WC1H 0AL

www.ucl-ioe-press.com

British Library Cataloguing in Publication Data:
A catalogue record for this publication is available from the British Library

ISBNs
978-1-85856-698-6 (paperback)
978-1-85856-805-8 (PDF eBook)
978-1-85856-806-5 (ePub eBook)
978-1-85856-807-2 (Kindle eBook)

Every effort has been made to trace copyright holders and to obtain their permission for the use of copyright material. The publisher apologizes for any errors or omissions and would be grateful if notified of any corrections that should be incorporated in future reprints or editions of this book.

The opinions expressed in this publication are those of the author and do not necessarily reflect the views of the UCL Institute of Education, University College London.

Typeset by Quadrant Infotech (India) Pvt Ltd
Printed by CPI Group (UK) Ltd, Croydon, CR0 4YY

Cover image © goodluz/Shutterstock.com

Contents

List of tables

List of figures

This book is dedicated to my family – Philip, James and Charlotte – and to all of the women who have shared their stories of juggling higher education studies and family life.

Acknowledgements

My utmost thanks and appreciation go to the women who have made this study possible. Through their willingness to share their higher education (HE) journeys with me and introduce me to their families, I have been able to gain some insights into juggling family life and identity change for mature women students. Their unwavering interest and belief in this study have humbled me and encouraged me to represent their stories as sincerely as I could. All names in this book have been changed to protect the identity of the women and their families.

This book is based on my Doctorate in Education thesis. I am very grateful to my supervisors, Dr Ulrike Hohmann and Dr Verity Campbell-Barr, for their unwavering commitment to helping me shape and construct my original research, and for their constructive criticism, advice, knowledge and guidance. Their constant encouragement and their ability to stretch and challenge me, even when I had self-doubts, have enabled me to have the confidence to research the lives of women students and their families. Also, to Dr Gillian Klein: this book would not have been possible without her dedication and time, and her belief that the stories here are worthy of being shared with a wider audience.

Finally, my thanks must also be extended to my ever-patient family who have lived with a wife and mother who studies. To my daughter Charlotte, whose encouragement has fostered my self-belief and given me motivation to continue with my studies. To my son James, whose laidback attitude and personal educational achievements have enabled me to see that anything is possible. Lastly to my husband Philip, who inspired me to start this journey of self-fulfilment and believed that I had the capability to achieve success. He has always encouraged and supported me in being a mum who studies. We have all seen from first-hand experience that having a mother who studies is not easy, but with support from the whole family we have achieved this together.

Betty's story

I began my study with apprehension, my self-esteem and self-worth was at rock bottom having been out of work for four years, and I was fully immersed in my role as a mum to my two young children, and not to mention my ongoing battle with postnatal depression. I also had to battle with my feelings of 'neglect' for my two young children when I started the degree, feelings of guilt at withdrawing myself from their 'beck and call'. My initial apprehension of studying soon diminished when I realized that early childhood studies was something I was motivated and passionate about. My confidence and self-esteem began to grow as I realized that this was something I was fairly good at, the studying and the work-based learning, immersing myself in a work role again.

Although I still felt guilty about not spending as much time with my son and daughter, a friend and fellow student, who was in the same 'boat' so to speak, gave me a different perspective, in that full-time studying was just like working, and parents work to better enable them to care and provide for their children. Them having a mummy who had a greater feeling of self-worth would indeed benefit the children. She made me realize that my feelings of guilt were misplaced. Indeed, the children benefited greatly. I will always remember a teacher at my son's school telling me how he had been constantly telling his friends that his mummy was at 'big school' and she was going to be a teacher, and she was taken aback by the pride that he was showing for what I was doing. My son, who was almost 6 at that time, started to bring pens and paper to the table I was studying at, writing stories and asking me about some of the 'big words' I was using, then relaying these words, scribbled on a post-it note with the definitions, in class with his friends and teachers.

My husband became a more practical dad than he had previously been, not that he was a bad dad in any way before, it's just the playing, occupying and caring was done by myself previously. After all, my role had been a full-time mum. The children weren't too keen to begin with, clinging onto me and crying when he tried to take them off for the day. On reflection about this time, I now see that this wasn't healthy; they relied on me for everything and my husband was neglected, unintentionally, by both our children and myself. Now we share care, but also make a point of weekends as family time. We are now a stronger family unit, and consciously spend quality time together. My parents, who had reservations about studying being too much for me, are openly proud of my achievements when speaking with their friends, something they have never done before. And I feel proud that I did it without their help, and proved them and others wrong. My husband has always been proud of me, but me having more self-worth and self-esteem has benefited our relationship hugely. I can remember being told at the start of my studies that full-time study will either break a marriage or will make it stronger. Maybe because I was conscious of this being a very real situation, I made sure that it worked, and this made us stronger. I can't imagine where we would be now, if it was not for me studying for my degree, and I wouldn't change a thing.

Introduction

My confidence has definitely grown throughout the course because I'm doing it, I still have to pinch myself and think I never got a degree when I left school and I'm actually doing it now and it's probably harder to do it now when you've got children and work and everything but when I say that to myself I do think, 'Yeah I can do this!'

(Angelina)

Who is this book for?

If you are starting or in the middle of higher education (HE) as a woman student with a family, then this book is for you. Starting HE as a woman with a family can be a complex, challenging and daunting task. When you are partway through your degree you can feel isolated from your family or under pressure and stress as you try to juggle the competing needs of your family, HE study and also possible work commitments. This book recognizes the strain that this puts on you and your family, and draws on insights gained from a research study based on women's experiences in order to offer practical strategies and advice to help you with your HE journey.

The book is aimed predominately at mature women students on HE programmes but is also of relevance to their partners and families as well as university lecturers and policymakers. Those who are starting out on HE programmes and want to consider the impact that HE might have on family life will be interested in the themes of the book. Those who are struggling with HE and juggling the many facets of their lives may identify with many of the characters. This book illuminates the journey of HE, the identity transformation and the effects on family life for the mature women participants in this study, as well as for some of their partners and children. It offers a blend of exploration of women's experiences, by relating them to the research findings, and practical strategies to support you during your HE experiences.

My HE experience

My work over the last ten years has been principally with mature women students returning to study, as I previously managed a higher education foundation degree programme in Early Childhood Studies in a further education (FE) college, and currently lecture in a university. Research subjects are often chosen due to their personal significance for the researcher (Etherington, 2004) and my own experiences as a mature student and mother are an integral part of this study. I can identify with the emotions women experience when entering HE, such as differing levels of self-confidence, guilt over family issues and juggling time. In my own personal family relationships, my HE study has been seen as a positive experience for the children and I have been positioned in and outside the family as successful, inspiring and worthy of admiration. However, coupled with this have been the financial pressures of studying, the negative impact of study on family time and the tensions that occurred as I have changed and developed my viewpoints on different topics. My HE study experiences and lecturing role have led me to consider one particular issue that affects female mature students: how a woman's increasing self-confidence and knowledge acquisition can change her, and can subsequently change her position in her relationships. The hypothesis that I keep coming back to is that support from a partner is often crucial to a woman's success.

I have observed women withdraw from an HE programme because of pressure from their partner and guilt over neglecting their family. Also, many of the women in this research have noted changes in themselves as they have adapted to university life. They discuss how their values, ideas and even conversations often change, thus putting pressure on their long-term relationship. Some partners appear to struggle with this change, particularly if they feel they are getting 'left behind', or being required to take a greater share of the childcare or household tasks. In contrast, I have also heard women talk positively about the support they have received from their partners, citing emotional support, help with the practical aspects of the course (for instance, proofreading, collecting library books, binding work), as well as help with childcare so that they could study.

This book has resulted from my research with women like myself. When I discuss my findings with women students they often exclaim, 'I thought it was just me that felt like this!' So the aim of this book is to illuminate these stories, so that women students can feel that they are not on their own and that their experiences are shared by many others.

Research themes

The aim of my research was to investigate the impact of HE on a woman's identity and family relationships, with mature female HE student participants from a foundation degree programme in Early Childhood Studies. The themes of identity change and family relationships that I investigated are explored in the shape of narratives told by the women students. These themes are common to all students, not just those on Early Childhood Studies programmes. Positioning myself as a mature woman student, mother and wife gives me insight into this topic and locates me firmly in the research process.

All research participants were mothers of children under the age of 18 years and all were either working or volunteering in Early Years settings.

Part One

Setting the scene

1

I was encouraged to start higher education, I think I was encouraged, I think one of my colleagues that I worked with, she was an incredibly inspirational woman, a very strong woman, no nonsense, absolutely no nonsense at all. And she just said to me, 'When are you going to go off and do your teaching, you should do it, you can do it', you know. She was the one that made me think, maybe; actually, maybe I should do it.

(Doris)

Part One considers previous research studies regarding the context in which mature women decide to embark on HE programmes, which results in a juggling act between HE studies and family life. The nature of changing identity, transformation and impact on family life is considered from the perspectives of the women. This leads into a brief introduction to the research underpinning the book, explaining the choice of methods and more importantly introducing the women participants on whom this book is centred.

Chapter 1

Background to mature women juggling HE study and family life

I still go back to the thing that I'm being selfish because that is how I see it you know because I was already a mother and this, that and the other and contributing to the household income, but you know why shouldn't I do this for myself? Why shouldn't I have a job that I really love and a career ahead of me, if I can balance it all and keep everybody happy and that's kind of what I hold to myself is that you know I need to do this for myself and why shouldn't I? You know I'm working hard, as long as everyone's happy and I'm doing what I should be doing then why not?

(Angelina)

Mothers accessing HE programmes often experience difficulty with balancing the competing demands of their family, work and study life (see Edwards, 1993a; Merrill, 1999; Parr, 2000; Pascall and Cox, 1993). In my teaching experience with mature women Early Childhood Studies foundation degree students, I have observed that studying often leads to changes in a woman's identity and family relationships as a whole. Below, I introduce three key themes that set the scene for this book: the background concerning women seeking HE, the change and transformation resulting from HE and the impact on the family when mothers study at HE level.

Women seeking higher-level qualifications

Previous studies on women students have named caring responsibilities and the conflicting role of being both mother and student as barriers to learning (Green Lister, 2003; Griffiths, 2002; Heenan, 2002). Regarding both the family and education as 'greedy institutions' in terms of time seems to be a common theme (Edwards, 1993a; Hughes, 2002). This is particularly relevant for mothers (Reay, 2003), as they are often considered responsible for organizing their study around the care needs of the family (Edwards,

1993a; Heenan, 2002). Women often feel guilt over studying and try to ensure that neither their family nor their educational study suffers because of the other (Merrill, 1999). The guilt comes from feeling that they are neglecting their family or their role as mother because they are fulfilling their own dreams. They can feel selfish for doing so; this makes them feel even guiltier. Before the research study, the women had talked to me as their tutor about their feelings of guilt, time pressures and balancing family, work and study needs. The same topics were often mirrored in their reflective journal writing, where they tried to make sense of how to support their family, work and make time for study.

This book focuses on women rather than men studying in HE, because studying as a mother is complex and made challenging by feelings of guilt, time pressures and conflicting roles. Through my own experiences of juggling the difficulties of studying and family life and through my observations of women students, I have witnessed how a woman's identity can change and develop during academic study.

If studying is so difficult for mothers, why do they do it? Research by Osgood (2006) gave the personal motivations for pursuing professional training and higher qualifications as being about gaining self-confidence and developing workplace professionalism. Education makes students more reflective, which can in turn lead them to challenge and critique their own professional practice (Cherrington and Thornton, 2013).

Although there are professional and personal benefits for women in HE study, it can be costly, as it is both emotionally and financially draining (Osgood, 2006). Women often have to deal with the guilt of studying and juggling their family's needs. And there will be financial implications, not only the tuition fees but also the loss of potential earnings. So embarking on an HE programme is not an easy decision.

Change and transformation as a result of HE

Identity transformation as a result of HE is a key theme both for the women in this study and for those featured in previous studies (Biesta *et al.*, 2011; Edwards, 1993a; Merrill, 1999; Parr, 2000; Pascall and Cox, 1993; Schuller *et al.*, 2004). But what is identity and why is it so relevant to women who study?

I see identity as something that is shaped and formed by the social environment (Taylor and Spencer, 2004), rather than the unchanging essence of a person (Jenkins, 2008). Like Burr (2003), I visualize identity as being made up of several different parts (see Figure 1.1 for some examples).

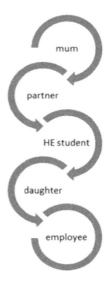

Figure 1.1: Different parts of an HE woman student's identity

For many of the women in this study, identity is seen through the roles they play, such as being a mum, a partner, an HE student, a daughter and an employee. They also use the word identity to describe the type of person they are; for example, whether they are quiet, kind, shy or confident. Everything the women thought about their identity changed during the course of their HE programme.

For the women considered in previous research studies, gender and motherhood were key parts of their identity. Women are portrayed as being constrained by their gender in terms of previous educational opportunities and socially constructed ideals of career opportunities for women (Pascall and Cox, 1993; Merrill, 1999). For some women students, their experiences at secondary school were negative or they were not encouraged by their parents to pursue higher-level qualifications (Pascall and Cox, 1993). Opportunities for work were restricted by socially constructed ideas of the women's role of domesticity and care for the family. These studies (Edwards, 1993a; Merrill, 1999; Parr, 2000; Pascall and Cox, 1993) described women as lacking choices, being passive and dominated by limited opportunities due to their gender. Education has changed since these studies and opportunities to progress to college have opened up. Now 46 per cent of men and 54 per cent of women enter further education. More women are taking the opportunity to progress into HE: statistics in 2013 show there were 8 per cent more women than men in full-time study and 20 per cent more women than men in part-time study (ONS, 2013).

For the majority of the women in these studies, the main source of their identity (before HE) was motherhood (Parr, 2000; Pascall and Cox, 1993). Although many women enjoy motherhood (see Pascall and Cox, 1993), it may not fulfil all aspects of their life and they can be actively seeking something more. Some women will not consider HE until the children are older and make fewer demands on their time and attention, delaying their application to study at HE level until they feel in a position to fit it around the needs of the family (Pascall and Cox, 1993). Edwards' study (1993a) found, in contrast, that children could adapt to the mother studying better than her partner did and were resilient and open to change, thus making redundant the mother's concerns about how the children would cope. Merrill's (1999) study was the only piece of research that compared the experience of men and women in HE. None of the men in this study cited domestic obligations or looking after children as an obstacle, whereas women with children saw family responsibilities as a barrier to their learning.

A number of studies have found that HE study can result in significant transformative changes to a woman's identity (Edwards, 1993a; Merrill, 1999; Pascall and Cox, 1993; Parr, 2000; Schuller *et al.*, 2004; Biesta *et al.*, 2011). Learning is inseparable from identity changes since the personal transformations women undergo occur as a result of their educational experience (see Edwards, 1993a and Biesta *et al.*, 2011). It is really hard for women to suppress the changes HE brings about. When HE changes how they see themselves, gives them confidence and new perspectives, it spills over into all aspects of their lives. This is natural and to be expected. It is explored in Part Two as we consider how women change their concept of themselves and how this has an impact on their relationships.

These transformations affect how women perceive themselves, or place themselves, as mothers and as partners. The women in studies such as those by Edwards (1993a) and Schuller *et al.* (2004) described the positive impact that HE had on themselves as they achieved higher self-esteem. This gives women increased confidence to demand more from their relationships and to want more for themselves. Being a student gives them a sense of prestige and status, which they may not have experienced as partners or mothers. It sets them apart from other mothers as they look at life and society from a changed perspective (Edwards, 1993a). Values, attitudes and behaviours shift and they gain a new awareness of themselves (Merrill, 1999), and are able to be more analytical (Edwards, 1993a).

The women's shifting knowledge base and increased self-confidence seep into the different areas of their lives, such as their children's education, family relationships and work situations (Edwards, 1993b; Schuller *et al.*,

2004). They feel more confident to influence their child's education and become more involved because of their developing knowledge base and identity. Their perceived raised status, due to their HE, gives them a self-confidence to speak to professionals and challenge issues, where they previously lacked self-confidence.

There are two main reasons why women change so dramatically when on an HE programme. Firstly, women seek out an HE programme because they are actively looking for a change. Secondly, through engagement with the course material, the women's beliefs and perspectives are transformed as they rethink previous assumptions and beliefs and reflect on them (Cherrington and Thornton, 2013; Mezirow, 2000).

Despite the benefits of entering an HE programme there is an issue of concern. Although pastoral support and HE are more accessible to mature students nowadays, withdrawals are still commonplace. As I see in my role as a tutor and lecturer to women students, this appears to be due to damage to family relationships and the excessive impact of study on time and family commitments (Snape and Finch, 2006).

Impact on the family

Mothers in HE often have to deal with demands that don't trouble other students, such as employment, childcare, household tasks, issues with time management and family pressures (Jamieson *et al.*, 2009; Reay, 2003). As argued by Hughes (2002), such pressures are often unique to women because of the historical and cultural assumptions that women will take on different social and family positions than male students (Plageman and Sabina, 2010). Mothers often take on the main responsibilities of childcare and household tasks.

Housework and childcare responsibilities do not decrease when women begin studying at HE level; rather their HE study becomes yet another component added into their lives. Men's and women's roles regarding childcare and household tasks are often perceived as unequal (Fatherhood Institute, 2016). Oakley (2005) presents a view of women's and men's lives and choices being different, based on her study in the 1970s of how housework and motherhood can limit the career and personal aspirations of mothers and deplete their identity. Although many more women today combine employment with family life (see DfE, 2013; Hughes, 2002; Reynolds *et al.*, 2003), there are still reports that responsibilities for housework (McFall, 2012) or childcare (EHRC, 2009) are unequal. According to research by the Institute for Social and Economic Research (McFall, 2012), women spend on average 15.4 hours on housework a week compared with men's 5.8 hours. Men are reported to spend only 24 minutes out of every hour that a woman spends caring for children (Fatherhood Institute, 2016). Despite an increase in women's participation in employment over the last 30 years (EHRC, 2009), many women still retain responsibility for childcare and domestic tasks (Doucet, 2006; EHRC, 2009; Fatherhood Institute, 2016).

As women cope with the 'greedy institutions' of both family and education (Edwards 1993a; Hughes, 2002), the problem of being 'time poor' (Edwards, 1993a) can cause strain if the father is expected to take on some of the childcare or household responsibilities. This is particularly complex in traditionally gender-split households where the mother has the main responsibilities for childcare and housework. Renegotiating the woman's role as mother and 'housekeeper' can add to stress, conflict and demands on her relationship. She may also feel emotional turmoil, torn between being a student and being a mother, as decision-making for mothers is primarily centred on the needs of the family rather than themselves (Williams, 2004). Sometimes the changes are embraced by the family and seen as positive but there is still a period of readjustment, as family life and relationships are modified.

As women's self-confidence, perspectives and lifestyle change, this can affect family dynamics, causing conflict and upset, as well as readjustment and compromise (Green Lister, 2003). Through learning and developing their knowledge base as a student, women are catapulted into a very different world. As they begin to rethink their values and perspectives, this can trigger friction in family and wider relationships (Green Lister, 2003). These changes cause identity transformation. I have observed women students struggling with their changing position as mother (see also Marandet and Wainwright, 2010; Reay, 2003), partner or employee, which is very different to that of being a student on an HE programme.

When women transform, they begin to question their identity, perspectives and family relationships but also their decision to study. Contemplating whether starting HE is the best decision is unsettling. Stepping into academic studies is like crossing a border of uncertainty into unknown territory. The territory of academia may feel very different and not necessarily within their reach. Women students from a workplace background often see their professional identity in terms of having vocational and practical skills. Reconsidering themselves academically as able to analyse theories or policies they previously took at face value can be exciting but challenging too. Walkerdine's research (2006) focused on the difficulties of waiting at the border between two quite different, and sometimes competing, ways of life. Sometimes a woman student may feel she does not quite belong in her previous identity as a mother, partner and worker, or in her newly constructed identity as mother, partner, worker and HE student. She is comfortable in neither the old role of mother and partner nor in the new role of HE student. These transformations to themselves, to family relationships and routines can come as a surprise to both the women and their families.

To manage the changes in relationships caused by HE study, some women develop strategies of either connecting or separating their studies from their partners (Edwards, 1993a). To acknowledge and try to make sense of changes in identity and family relationships, Edwards used the ideas of Gilligan (1982, cited by Edwards, 1993a) to explain her connecting theory, claiming that a woman's identity is intrinsically linked to relationships with others. Edwards (1993a) developed three categories: connecting study with home, separating education and family, and the mix of both connecting and separating education and family (see Table 1.1).

Some of the women in the connectors group said that their knowledge gain was viewed by their partners as a threat to their relationship. This caused conflict, and a quarter of these relationships ended. Other factors that might have contributed to their relationship breaking down were not considered. The women were not fixed in a single category, however, as women moved along the separator and connector scales during their course. Some became separators because the connecting was not working and so they changed their strategy to save or ease their relationship. This resonated with my own story and experiences. I could trace my journey from connecting, to separating, to connecting, back to separating, depending on what level of conflict or encouragement I was receiving from my family. Such shifting is a survival mechanism and a way of managing the competing demands of study and family life. Chapter 5 explores how women use the approaches of connecting and separating their studies to develop strategies to aid them in juggling HE and family life.

Clearly, these research studies show that juggling family life and HE study is not a new issue for women students. Women face many barriers to learning. Nevertheless, they want to complete an HE programme for professional and personal reasons. Changes to family life are a consequence of HE study. As women transform and change their perspectives, this rubs off on the family and family routines change to accommodate to their study.

Table 1.1: Separating or connecting HE studies and family life

Category	Description	Examples
• **Connectors –** connecting study (52% of women, Edwards, 1993a)	Trying to connect home (partners, children) with student life and study. These women are not able to separate their identities into student, partner or mother and see themselves as one complete person. However, this can be seen as a threat to some relationships and is not always welcomed by a partner.	• Sharing university experiences and issues with coursework at home • Discussing university topics • Introducing HE friends to family or taking family to the university to introduce them to her new environment • Studying openly at home
• **Separators** – separating education and family (19% of women, Edwards, 1993a)	Viewing student and home identities as completely separate. Some women do not wish to connect home and study in any way and enjoy their own personal space and the privacy of keeping both spheres separate. This separation is important for some women as they see education as bringing an individual identity for themselves as a student, which is disconnected from family life, rather than the more public shared identity of mother or partner (Parr, 2000).	• Minimal discussion at home regarding university experiences • Hiding study from family: either studying at university or studying when the children are in bed • Not allowing the study books to take over the home • Not discussing any HE challenges or difficulties at home

Category	Description	Examples
• **Mixers** – mixing connections and separations of education and family (29% of women, Edwards, 1993a)	Some women are both connectors and separators for different aspects and see 'switching hats' as the only way of dealing with the demands of both spheres.	• Using a range of the strategies above depending on which takes the priority at the time (e.g. family or study) and dependent on the changing needs of different family relationships

Source: Edwards (1993a).

What this book does is present a combination of research findings and practical strategies to help you juggle your HE studies with your family life. This sets it apart from other research studies. It intersperses research from the women with comments to you as the woman student and concludes with practical strategies to support you through your course. The experiences and stories of many women students studying at HE level enable you to understand and reflect on your own. The book draws on the experiences of women students who were generally in traditionally gendered households. When their HE studies commenced, the mothers still had the main responsibility for childcare and household chores.

Chapter 2 introduces the methods employed in this study and the women studied, summing up their stories of transformation and the effects on their family. Readers might find there is one character they most identify with, and follow her story, experiences and comments throughout the book.

Introducing the women and the research methods

I spoke to women in an FE college studying an Early Childhood Studies foundation degree, and what they told me relates to all women students with families. However, the research gave me a restricted sample of white, British women, who were almost all in largely traditionally gendered heterosexual relationships. They were selected from students who were on or had just completed a foundation degree programme, so their experiences of study were still current (see Table 2.1 for further details of the students and their families).

The small sample size allowed me to collect in-depth stories that offer a contextual picture or snapshot in time, and meant I could delve deeper into the personal stories of each woman using multiple methods to construct an in-depth qualitative study. Using a small sample of women enabled me to illuminate the richness of their stories as a whole and gave me breadth in the findings.

Table 2.1: Table of participants

Female student	Partner	Programme information	Child 1	Child 2	Child 3	Child 4
Female students whose partners were male participants in the study						
Angelina, aged 38	Bradley	Second year, part-time student	Alex, aged 9	Alice, aged 5	–	–
Esme, aged 55	Alan	Second year, part-time student	Emily, aged 17	–	–	–
Maggie, aged 48	Ross	Second year, part-time student	Rob, aged 21	Henry, aged 19	Claire, aged 16	Lin, aged 13

Female student	Partner	Programme information	Child 1	Child 2	Child 3	Child 4
Female students whose partners were not included in the study						
Betty, aged 35	Lloyd	First year student (interrupted her studies due to childcare issues)	Matthew, aged 5	Sophie, aged 3	–	–
Christina, aged 42	Dominic	Third year degree top-up, part-time student	Jack, aged 17	Anna, aged 15	–	–
Doris, aged 41	David	Second year, full-time student	Isobel, aged 9	Fiona, aged 8	–	–
Heidi, aged 33	Joe	Third year degree top-up, full-time student	Ellie, aged 9	Sam, aged 6	Mandy, aged 5	–
Hilary, aged 42	–	First year, full-time student	Imogen, aged 5	George, aged 5	–	–
Jennifer, aged 37	Jon	First year, part-time student	Ella, aged 9	Ben, aged 7	Megan, aged 4	
Kim, aged 27	Matt	Third year degree top-up, full-time student	Colin, aged 9	James, aged 7	Izzy, aged 4	–
Marie, aged 41	Harry (separated while on course)	First year, full-time student	Katie, aged 14	Oscar, aged 6	–	–

Introducing the participants
Angelina and Bradley

> I was the typical wife in that I took on every single part of the woman's role, or what is perceived as the woman's job in the

> house, all the cleaning, in fact this changed massively, all the
> cleaning, all the cooking, and all the housework.
>
> (Angelina)

Angelina is a 38-year-old childminder, who has been married to Bradley
for 12 years. Bradley is a director of a web company and has a level 4
qualification. They have two children aged 5 and 9. As a result of Angelina's
HE experiences, she became more confident and driven. She is now able
to see things from multiple perspectives, which have enabled her to see
life differently and analyse situations more reflectively. Although Angelina
believed this analytical approach caused some issues with her partner
initially, this was resolved when they realized what Angelina could achieve
in terms of career progression with the degree. Bradley has taken over a large
share of household and childcare tasks in order to give Angelina enough
time to study. Both Angelina and Bradley feel that Bradley's support has
contributed to her success and the children helped as they were supportive
and accommodating.

Esme and Alan

> Learning at this level and knowing how hard it is has sort of
> occupied me … So it's taken me away from, quite a lot of my
> concentration … I feel I have not been as supportive as a mum. As
> a partner, I think it's just gone completely off the radar *(laughter)*.
> Yeah … I don't think I was there.
>
> (Esme)

Esme is a 55-year-old family support worker in a children's centre. She has
been in a relationship with Alan for 23 years and has one daughter aged
17, living at home. Alan is a full-time police officer and had experience of
HE himself, completing a degree 17 years ago. While on the programme,
Esme discovered that she had dyslexia. This was a major identity shift,
once she realized that she was a not a 'lesser person' as she had believed,
and this enabled her to acknowledge her own abilities. She now feels more
knowledgeable and feels that her better understanding has enhanced all of
her relationships, because she can look at things in depth from a theoretical
viewpoint. Initially, her relationship with Alan suffered. She felt that she
concentrated so fully on her studies she had nothing left of herself to give
her partner. However, this resolved itself during the programme and Alan's
encouragement and help with proofreading her work were invaluable. Alan
was very positive about Esme's studies as he believed that HE was a valid
tool in self-development.

Maggie and Ross

> Ross has definitely helped on a practical level ... if he hadn't upped his game in terms of what he has done, I couldn't have done it ... well I just couldn't have, you know. He really was, he has been amazing and he hasn't griped and he hasn't moaned ... he has just quietly got on and done things [housework and cooking].
>
> (Maggie)

Maggie is a 48-year-old nursery manager. She has been married to Ross for the past 24 years and has four children aged between 13 and 21. Maggie's identity prior to HE was centred solely on being a mother, housewife and choosing a career path or job that fitted around her children's needs. As the course progressed, Maggie grew in self-confidence and knowledge. She described herself as having a 'presence' and being an educational example to her children. She benefited from strong support from her partner, Ross, who took on many of the household, childcare and cooking tasks. Maggie saw him as instrumental in her success on the degree. Ross believed that it would be difficult for a woman to study at HE level without a supportive partner who was willing to adjust to accommodate her study needs. Ross also saw his son as being an important factor in his partner's success through the educational support and camaraderie he provided as they were both studying in HE at the same time.

Betty

> Who am I doing this for? I'm doing it for me to try and build myself back up but then it's had a negative effect on Sophie [daughter] really. I was kind of like a little bit torn and it was all getting a little bit too much for me. I was sat upstairs studying and getting stressed out thinking, 'I've got to get this done so that I can be with Sophie'. I always knew the day that I withdrew from the course that this is not the end, I'm going to come back.

Betty is a 35-year-old full-time mum, who volunteers at a pre-school setting. She has been married to Lloyd for seven years and has two children aged 5 and 3. Betty described her identity before motherhood as being located in her work, which gave her status. She felt that she lost this status when she became a mother and also suffered from postnatal depression. Starting HE made her proud and her self-esteem grew as she found she could balance motherhood and studying towards her career goals. But her daughter failed to settle at nursery, and Betty's parents withdrew their childcare support as they believed the course was putting too much pressure on her and her family. Betty did receive some childcare support from her partner, which enabled her to study from home, but her guilt over her daughter not settling at nursery, coupled with the lack of support from her parents, made her withdraw from the course. Betty returned to the course the following autumn after spending the year preparing her daughter for the transition.

Christina

> No, he [partner] never in any way asked me to stop [studying], what he did do was say, 'Are you sure you are alright? You know it's not the be all and the end all', and I said, 'Yes' ... I used to think, 'Oh my goodness, I'm not going to pass, I am not at the right academic level', in those first few assignments and he was saying, 'Yes, you can, you can do it'.

Christina is a 42-year-old pre-school leader, who has been married to Dominic for 21 years and has two children aged 15 and 17. Dominic is a company director. Christina described her identity prior to HE as a pre-school leader, daughter, daughter-in-law, sister, wife and mother. Through being on the degree programme, her confidence in her own abilities and her ability to complete assignments increased. Her identity started changing as she realized that she did know what she was talking about (confidence in 'knowing'), she felt more reflective both at work and at home, and her self-esteem increased through assignment successes. Christina believes that her children learnt to cook and be more independent because she was busier with HE. They also learnt to go to their father for help rather than relying so greatly on her. Christina believes that she could not have coped with HE without the support of her partner and family.

Doris

> David [partner] has seen me change, and he has really struggled with this kind of confident person now.

Doris is a 41-year-old teaching assistant, who has been married to David for 11 years. She has two children aged 8 and 9. David is a carpenter and has a level 3 qualification. Doris described her identity before HE as 'lacking in self-confidence' and 'not feeling as good as other people'. She described herself as a 'mouse' that hid behind her partner. During HE she became confident as she began achieving high grades and felt ready emotionally, psychologically and physically to branch out to new avenues.

Feeling differently about herself and her new self-confidence has affected her relationship with her partner. She no longer feels she has to hide behind him and actually believes that she is more confident than he is. This shift, plus the time commitments of HE study, caused friction at first. She believes that he found it difficult to adapt to her more confident and independent self. Doris's daughters appreciated what she was doing and they understood why she did not spend quite as much time with them, but knew when they needed her she would always put them first. Her daughters learnt to play independently and took pride in what she was achieving.

Doris's experiences highlight how a mature student's self-confidence can change both personally in their feelings and socially in their actions, in quite a transformative way. Doris linked the changes to educational success. Doris described herself as a 'little mouse' before she undertook HE, letting her partner take the lead in social situations where she appeared quiet and 'invisible'. She located her lack of self-confidence in her experiences as a child 'born out of wedlock'. For her, this was an important part of her identity: she felt 'not as good as other people' and 'looked down on' by others. This affected her self-confidence at school and, although she felt the teachers believed in her academic abilities, Doris doubted herself and felt 'held back' by her background and lack of self-confidence and self-belief:

> The teachers at school always used to say to me, 'You are going to go on and do something', and I thought, 'No, not me, I will never make anything of myself', so that held me back.

Doris's confidence in her own ability grew slowly over time, and she related it to her success in assignment work:

> I know I am the kind of person that will always feel like I am 'not good enough', always the underdog and only worthy of praise when I am achieving to a very high standard.
>
> (Year 1 journal entry)

> Because I think through doing the degree, it is almost that I had to prove to myself that I was worthy ... I was so scared that I was going to fall flat on my face, I'm not going to be able to do this ... I think I've got 57 per cent on my first piece [assignment] and I'm so proud of myself ... I proved myself that I was capable of learning all of those new skills ... I actually feel proud of what I am doing.

This self-confidence spilled over into other aspects of her life as she felt 'more confident and able'. This had an impact on her relationship with her partner and Doris sensed that the power dynamics in their relationship had changed:

> I was much less confident than what I am now, umm, I always felt that I wasn't as good as other people ... So probably, I am quite the confident one now, in many ways he [partner] is the one that is not quite as confident when you scratch the surface a little bit.

Heidi

> I was a mother and that was my life ... I think you learn once you start your degree and you learn so much more about things and I think, ummm, this does then influence [parenting] ... and I thought I've got this opportunity now to do this while the children are younger ... Time was a huge factor, for them as well, because I did not have as much time to spend with them, like I've done before.

Heidi is a 33-year-old full-time mother and volunteer at a local primary school. She is married to Joe, a landscape gardener, and has three children aged 5, 6 and 9. Before HE, she defined her identity in motherhood and explained that this was 'her life'. She changed from being fully attentive and available for her children to being a mother who was balancing her time between the children and study. She felt the course had affected how she parented as she is now more aware of her children's developmental needs. During the foundation degree, she prioritized time to help them with their schoolwork. She feels her perspectives are much broader now and she is constantly reflecting and questioning herself. This has led her to be less judgemental, calmer and a lot more confident. Her identity shifts and changed parenting style have rubbed off on her partner, Joe, and he too has developed a calmer and more reflective approach.

Hilary

> I will always put me as a mum first ... I have a lot of frustration, as I do not give the foundation degree 100 per cent, but feel I am giving what I can. I could give more but what gives? ... I have to be happy with my choices.

Hilary is a 42-year-old single parent and volunteer at a pre-school. She has twins aged 5. She described her identity prior to HE as, 'A mum. I will always put me as a mum first.' Hilary has found that since HE she has changed her perspective. As she now looks at things in different ways, she feels more positive about herself. Hilary believes that this has benefited her children as her developing knowledge base and engagement with HE have added an additional element to her children's awareness of 'what is different in life'. As a single parent, Hilary is solely responsible for the care of her children. She feels she experiences more stress now, as she has more things on her mind and can lose patience more easily with her children. She feels frustration at balancing her time to study and be with the children. Because she can't give 100 per cent to her study, she believes that she is not achieving the grades she could, but she will not compromise on her time with the children. Hilary feels it is better to under-achieve and that she has no alternative as motherhood is her top priority. She receives no practical support and her family give her little emotional support. Hilary feels the greatest benefit of support has been from her tutor. Having a supportive tutor who has a flexible approach and who understands the complexities of juggling family and study life has really helped her.

Jennifer

> My main identity is a mum, that is my biggest responsibility … basically I have done everything for them, for the children, whilst Jon has been working … I was 'super housewife' me, cleaning, walking the dog, the shopping everything really, my husband does have to do slightly more, umm, because, when they [children] are sick he has to stay with them, because when they are sick and I have a college day, I have made him do it. So, he has had to step up a little more, he will do the shopping over the weekend.

Jennifer is a 37-year-old pre-school deputy manager. She has been married to Jon for 14 years and has three children aged 4, 7 and 9. Prior to HE, Jennifer described her main strand of identity as being a mum, as she viewed that as her biggest responsibility and always saw herself as putting others first. Jennifer has become more self-assured and self-confident since embarking on the HE course but has changed how she spends her time. Her time with the children has changed from playing with them and planning creative activities to being an educational role model and supporting them with their homework or issues at school. Jennifer has felt supported by her partner with the childcare and household tasks. She has also received practical support from her mother-in-law, although she has shown disapproval of Jennifer studying, believing she is neglecting her partner, children and duties at home. Jennifer has struggled with this disapproval, but believes that her partner has supported her over it.

Kim

> I'm parenting differently because I have got a much more in-depth understanding of children's needs ... I do naturally reflect on things quite a lot which means I think everything through ... certainly things have changed, definitely the roles, I haven't had time this year for things like housework and I don't know if this is a reflection of my own time management but I seem to have less time for everything and I have sort of stretched myself a lot this year and my husband has been doing ... so he does the housework and he's taken over most of those sorts of things whereas it used to be a joint thing.

Kim is a 27-year-old full-time mother and volunteer at a local nursery. She is married to Matt, manager of an IT department, and has three children aged 4, 7 and 9. Kim's identity prior to HE was tied to being a single mother. When she was younger, she felt this had reduced her standing in the local community. While on the programme, she became more knowledgeable about Early Years practices, and this unsettled her for a time as she grappled with the parenting decisions she had made earlier that she considered poor. However, the programme has taught her to be reflective, analytical and to see things from other perspectives. This has enabled her to resolve past difficulties because she understands issues in a new light. She believes her increased knowledge about Early Years has had an impact on both her and her partner's parenting practices and that her analytical skills have enhanced her relationship with her partner. She believes that completing her HE studies has raised her status both at home and socially. Kim has relied on her partner for additional childcare, support with her studies and general household tasks, which she thinks has put a strain on him but believes she could not have completed her foundation degree without his support.

Marie

> I kind of knew, when we [her and her partner] had a rocky bit in the first term ... because I was finding it very difficult as well. And we had a lot of debate over it, I sort of said, 'I will give it up [HE]', but within my heart of hearts I wasn't going to ... I have found something I feel I'm good at; I feel I'm doing well on the degree. I now have a massive determination to finish it, but not just finish it, finish it with style, I don't want to scrape it.

Marie is a 41-year-old mum who has recently separated from her partner Harry (since the beginning of term 2 of the course). Marie has two children aged 6 and 14. She located her identity prior to HE as someone who had never achieved any formal qualifications, always starting things but not completing them, and being tied into destructive relationships. She described the course as giving her self-confidence, self-esteem and enabling her to achieve autonomy again. Marie's philosophy as a mother has changed. Her parenting style is more relaxed and her approach is less cautious. Now she believes her children need risk and challenging opportunities. Marie has received support and encouragement from her children: they are proud of her achievements and celebrate her high grades. They play independently more often, giving her time to concentrate on her coursework.

Marie's identity change had an impact on the already problematic relationship with her partner, which then disintegrated. But she viewed this change as necessary and positive. As she said:

> I do feel like I'm a very, very, different person. I'm not sure Harry [partner] likes the person that I am now.

Before she tackled HE, Marie had a habit of not completing tasks or seeing things through to the end. She also tended to rely heavily on her partner, which diminished her self-confidence and self-esteem and created problems in her relationship:

> I had a dreadfully destructive relationship with Katie's [elder daughter] father … my self-respect and self-esteem here [points to mind map] were pretty low.

Her pattern of not completing qualifications or realizing career goals made her and her parents feel that she was a disappointment as she had not achieved her potential. This affected her identity, making her see herself as a failure:

> I have started and failed several things in my adult life … so you see, parental respect, I've never had it … They [parents] always think I have failed as I have never lived up to my potential.

Marie's negative relationships and lack of self-confidence made her feel that she could not take control over her life and be independent. Her identity was characterized by low self-confidence, low self-esteem and an over-reliance on others:

> I don't think I ever commanded myself, I always drifted … I'm a little bit shocked that a year down the line I am sticking something out!

Because of the HE-propelled transformation of her identity she distanced herself from her former role. Her partner neither shared her new perspective nor supported her identity change: one reason why the relationship ended. As Marie explained:

> I will not give up on the course and chose that over my marriage ... I have a changed perspective; I let the children have risk and challenge opportunities ... I am in a stronger place now ... my own self-respect has gone up, now I have my own drive ... I own my own space ... I am in charge of me.

Through HE Marie regained her independence, changed her philosophy on life and began to make decisions for herself again. She linked her change in identity and transformation to studying at HE level:

> I don't physically have enough time in the day to worry about anything like that, there is no negative space in my life ... It's all about me and the kids now ... Having a presence that says I've got pride in myself but I just feel like I've got my own personal space. I'm not scared of being alone anymore ... The course has given me the confidence to say you can do this, you can actually challenge yourself and you can succeed.

In summary, my qualitative research methods allowed for a flexible approach that encouraged the women to present narrative accounts of their experiences as students, mothers and partners. They afford a range of stories of how juggling HE studies has an impact on family life, ranging from hostility and little support, to changes in roles and shifts in status within a relationship. Extended stories from Doris and Marie are examples of a lack of support from a partner but they were the minority of my sample.

Although they cannot represent every woman's experiences of juggling HE and family life, the stories presented here do offer some insights into what can happen. The following chapter explores in more detail the types of transformations and changes women experience when they begin an HE programme.

Part Two

Self-transformation

I think the whole process of transformation that the course takes you through is amazing, because you do transform your whole depth of thinking through evaluation and all of the reflection. You just evolve with it, and when I know something now I believe that I know it.

(Maggie)

You can really see how I've travelled, you can see the changes and I think, I think the children would back that up.

(Marie)

I think that has actually made me look at things differently because I'm curious now, you know, I'm much more curious about why do we behave the way we do.

(Esme)

When you embark on an HE programme, transformation is to be expected. You probably chose your course because you want to develop your knowledge or understanding of a certain topic, or you want a change of career direction. Part Two explores the transformative effect of HE on women's identity, changing their belief systems, perspectives and behaviours. Such changes to identity and their impact on family relationships are described from the perspective of the women in my study and based on their accounts. Each woman's transformation is unique to her but in sharing the women's experiences I hope to provide insights into the effects of identity change on women students. At the end of each chapter that follows, I discuss the various strategies identified that support women while they are juggling studies and family life.

Chapter 3

The importance of being a good mum

I always wanted to be the best mum … I now have a good relationship with my children so I must have done something right.

(Esme)

Being a mum often feels like the most important aspect of a woman's life. When considering an HE course, the problem of how the family will cope with a mum who studies is often uppermost in a woman's mind. One of the main reasons why they may withdraw from an HE programme is often because juggling HE and family life just becomes too difficult. Balancing the needs of the children with the desire to study is never easy. It is no surprise then that motherhood featured most heavily in all of the women's accounts of their changing identity and the effects of HE on their family relationships (see Figure 3.1).

I was a mother and that was my life.

(Heidi)

My main identity is a mum, that's my biggest responsibility.

(Jennifer)

'I've always been a mum … actually this [HE] is for me'

Even women who enjoy full-time motherhood can reach a point where they want something more. The decision to study can be difficult as they feel guilty about saying that being a mum is not enough:

I think being at home all the time is lovely, but I think sometimes you need something else in your life.

(Heidi)

I was a mother, wife and daughter … I knew I hadn't found, well I had been in various jobs, none of which I really wanted to do.

(Angelina)

25

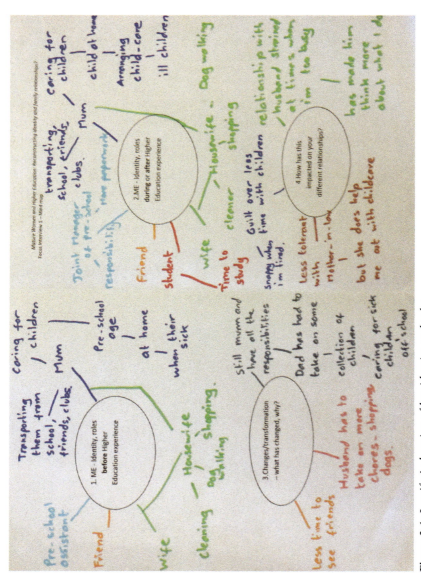

Figure 3.1: Jennifer's drawing of her identity and roles

Women tend to define being an effective mother in terms of how much time they are able to give to their children and the quality of their relationship. Being able to devote sufficient time to their children, whether this is juggling work and family or being a stay-at-home mother, is of utmost importance to women. All the women wanted to be able to study and still have time to play with their children, attend their sporting activities and provide love, support and care. In short, women want to be able to do it all but this means making concessions. One concession can be working part time:

> I always wanted to be a mum, it was my choice ... I chose to work part time so I could be there for my children.
>
> (Esme)

> I only worked part time and I was at home with the children, also I saw that as my place. My husband literally went to work, he earnt the money and came home and played with the children, so I was very much a housewife, mother and wife.
>
> (Angelina)

Here are two different perspectives on being a mother: *wanting* to fulfil the motherhood role and feeling that it was a role *allocated* to them. Betty, for example, felt that the role of mother was *allocated* to her, and she was torn between wanting to be at home and wanting to work, whereas Heidi felt content in her *chosen* role as a full-time mum.

Betty had a high-powered and rewarding job before she became a mother and, although she enjoyed being a mum, she did miss the status and buzz she got from her work:

> Yes I loved my job, I worked really long hours and I think because I worked the long hours and was so committed, that's why I worked my way up [promotion] so quickly ... I decided to start a family and within a year of getting married I had Matthew [son] and then it kind of went downhill a little bit then. Not because I had Matthew but just kind of me, in myself, I kind of lost everything that was me really ... then I had my little girl and that was quite stressful as well so my mood just got lower and lower because she was quite a hard baby in the beginning and I think I was already at a low point then and I suffered from postnatal depression and all of that and I have suffered with it quite badly ... and it has taken a long time to build myself up again and then I thought well alright Sophie is going to childcare

now so I thought I'm going to do this [HE]. I'm going to get my teeth stuck into something.

Betty thoroughly enjoyed her HE course at first but then her daughter became distressed whenever she attended university and she faced opposition from her parents, who remembered her postnatal depression and were concerned with how the course was affecting her stress levels. They wanted her to focus on 'being a mum again' and not neglect her 'duties' as a mother. This theme of parents' attitudes to HE is discussed in Chapter 6.

In contrast, Heidi loved being a mum and only chose HE as a way to help her children with their education and build a stronger financial future for them:

Ellie [daughter] had started school, I was really enjoying what she was doing and I was enjoying helping her, and then I thought, 'Gosh, as she is getting older she is going to be learning more and I am not going to be able to help her'. Also, I was very lucky because I didn't have to work when they were younger. I did part time for a little while, but then I had Sam, and then this stopped. I thought I'm going to have to go back to work at some point, and I don't want to have to go back to work in dental nursing, I want to do better than that, I want to go higher.

Heidi worried about leaving her children in order to study:

So, my life at that time? Well I was a mother and that was my life … I love being with them, it broke my heart when I had to take them to nursery, I came out of there in tears on the first day. Even when I was at university, I found that hard, really hard, the minute we were finished I was straight down to nursery to get them. That was the hardest thing that I had to deal with … I thought, perhaps she [daughter] was too young but it worked out quite well because it [university] was only two days a week so it wasn't like I was gone all week from them. And the rest of the time I was with them, well I say I was with them but studying like mad.

How a woman views her role as a mum affects how she feels about committing a lot of her time and focus to HE studies. When a mother feels fulfilled as the main carer (like Heidi), she may struggle with time away from the children while attending university or studying. Other mothers (like Betty) are looking for something in addition to their role as mother. Betty was looking for a change in status, which HE study gave her:

I thought I'm going to do this myself ... I kind of feel that when you are a stay-at-home mum, you know people ask you what you do, you say, 'Oh I stay at home, I'm a full-time mum', there is kind of like a stigma attached to it, it's you know, you are shirking your responsibilities to provide for the family really, so I felt quite proud that I was actually doing something ... I loved the fact that when people asked me what I did I said, 'Yes, I'm going back to university, I'm doing something'. It just kind of picked me up mood wise.

Becoming a mother who studies changes how women view themselves as a parent:

I don't want to stop studying and that is a really weird thing I think to feel, and that's a very different feeling for me as I've always put other people first. And so other people and what they need has always been more important than what I have needed, and this isn't necessarily what I need, this is what I want, and I really want this now. I'm not prepared to give it up, and I thought I'm going to do whatever it takes.

(Doris)

Before HE, women make choices that put their children's needs above their own needs for a career or self-satisfaction. HE study changes this.

Changing concepts of motherhood

I have changed as a mother since I've been on this course. My viewpoint of parenting has changed.

(Angelina)

Motherhood is viewed as a separate and distinctive role to fatherhood. All the mothers (with the exception of Kim) were in charge of household chores and looking after the children. Although they delegated some chores, the main responsibility for the housework remained with them. They saw being a mother and housewife as part of their identity, with clear and separate gendered roles from their partner. This is not uncommon for women when they start an HE programme. The roles appeared flexible enough to be switched to adapt to their study needs. Changing roles within the family, particularly the housework, is common for a woman student as she and her family realize that she can no longer do it all. Adapting women's roles is necessary so they can cope with the demands of study and family life. This is not possible for all women, for example single parents, or those whose partners are unable or unwilling to help with chores.

Putting the needs of their children first changes during the process of the HE programme. The students have to prioritize their own requirements and free up time to study or attend university. Heidi's story shows how it is possible to combine being a 'stay-at-home mum' and HE student:

> The amount of work that I had to do was so much that I was on the computer every other day ... Sometimes Sam [young son] would sit on my lap when he started getting tired and he would fall asleep on my lap while I was sat on the computer typing. I actually loved that time in the afternoon when he would go to sleep.

Heidi was able to balance the demands of motherhood and being a student, responding to her son's emotional and care needs alongside her studying. But she still worried about how her studying affected her family. She asked her daughter how it felt to have a mother who studies (also see Figure 3.2):

> My 9-year-old decided that she did remember me on the computer a lot working but she didn't mind me working on the computer because she knew it was going to get me a good job in the long run, so she seemed rather supportive of that. She made a point of saying that she loved her mum so whatever mum does is fine! All that fuss I was making rushing from college, running down the road to get to them at nursery as quick as I could was unnecessary. But they seemed quite happy and it's almost like they seem to understand why I am doing it and they don't mind which is really nice to hear. I was imagining from their point of view that it was worse than it was.

Figure 3.2 tells quite a story. Look at the computer and how large it is in the picture compared with the image of Heidi. The computer was perceived by Heidi's daughter as playing a big part in their everyday lives. This links with Heidi's comments earlier about frequently being 'on the computer' and her son falling asleep on her lap. Look at the size of the heart in the picture; this is giving a clear message to her mum. Despite the changes to routine (studying at home, additional nursery and childcare), her daughter still loved her and supported her HE studies.

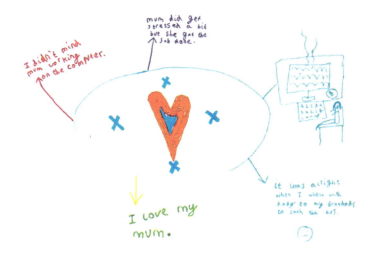

Figure written annotations:
- mum did get stressed a bit but she got the job done.
- I didn't mind mum working on the computer.
- I love my mum.
- it was alright when I went with daddy to my grandads to have the art.

Figure 3.2: Heidi's 9-year-old daughter's memories and account of her mum studying

So it is important to have a flexible approach to mothering (like Heidi) and to make compromises. Finding strategies to balance how you want to be as a mother and an HE student is really important. These strategies will be individual to you and based around your family's needs. Devising effective strategies will enable you to juggle the practicalities of arranging childcare, dealing with guilt and finding time to study. As a mum with an older child, Esme did not feel guilty about making her need to study a priority:

> I kept thinking I've got to do this for myself, I've always been a mum … actually this is for me.

Although motherhood is important for women students, it is a fluid and evolving part of who you are. As your self-image changes, so can your view of motherhood:

> I've always sat down and I've done activities with them [prior to HE], my house has always been like a pre-school as well … we always have the play dough out, the paint … I suppose that has had an impact as I haven't done as much as I feel I should … I have not had the time [now she is an HE student] … I now sit at one end of the table and my 9-year-old will get her homework and sit at the other and she feels like we are both working. So in that respect I think it's having an impact on her.
>
> (Jennifer)

31

Jennifer, like Heidi, changed her view of a mother as someone who always needs to be there to entertain and play with her children to someone who is able to study alongside them. Although she felt guilty about having less time with them, she saw how her studying gave her daughter a positive perspective on learning. When women study, their beliefs about what it is to be a good mother change with the different priorities and time pressures. Adapting to this can often mean a change in perspective about motherhood or a change in routine. Other aspects of identity will also change, and this is to be expected.

Changing parenting style

Some women found that the subjects they studied had an impact on their parenting. They began analysing their own practices as their knowledge base increased. They gained greater awareness of their children's needs and modified their parenting practices accordingly:

> Doing the course has made me more in-depth, I can now look at it from a more theoretical point of view ... I think that has helped me so I can analyse, you know, if my daughter is feeling down or whatever and I can think how can I handle this, so I can talk to her better and actually understand this is the stage she is going through. So I am meeting her needs better because I am more knowledgeable.
>
> (Esme)

Whatever programme of study women take up, they find that through HE they begin to develop a questioning style and an ability to look at things from multiple perspectives. When women study at HE level, they develop skills of analysis and critical thinking. They reflect on their parenting practices so they can make better decisions for their children. However, having greater knowledge can cause women to view past parenting decisions negatively and make them feel guilty:

> I understand their [children's] needs better and I understand their behaviour better and I understand my natural reaction a lot better, but that makes me feel really guilty because most of the time as a parent I think you react in the moment with the instinct ... whereas now and from that guilt I probably over-compensate so it does affect the way that I parent.
>
> (Kim)

When women change their perspectives they also challenge their own view of being a mother. This can lead to a period of imbalance or unrest or discomfort (Erichsen, 2011). This was apparent among the women as they struggled with their previous identity and the way it was changing. Rethinking who you are can be unsettling for those around you too, as everyone tries to adapt to the new you. But Kim saw this conflict as a positive process, with each module an opportunity to reflect on her old parenting practices. Before embarking on HE, Kim was a young single mother who had little support. It was a difficult time, both financially and emotionally. Kim believed that her HE studies helped her to be more reflective about her past:

> I was a young mum, I was quite young so I would have been 21, yeah I was 21 but I had two children at that point so although I was 21 I was still quite young because I hadn't sort of done any of those things that you do to grow up … So I did feel quite sort of lost and vulnerable … and the pressure of it, I don't think you realize at the time but sort of looking back on it I don't really know how I managed to cope with it because there are so many finances and benefits with it that I didn't really know what I was doing …. But I struggled quite a lot with being on my own and not really wanting to be a mum and not really having much support and when I read things now I usually get quite upset and I have struggled with a few of the modules where I have just not been able to move forward with it. So there were a few which were quite difficult but I do think that this [HE studies] has helped me work through my own things.

Although Kim is now in a supportive relationship, she believed that it was important to reflect back and compare her past and current experiences. The course content enabled her to question her parenting style and understand some of her earlier experiences. Through reconsidering her past and transforming her self-image, Kim felt that she had gained greater control over her life (Mezirow, 1991):

> From being a young parent and a single parent and all of those sort of difficult times that I have dealt with … every module that we have done has been a little bit of therapy as well … actually understanding some of the theory behind different aspects of things that I have been through has made it easier to understand things and let them go or resolve them … I have been able to let go some of those demons and things which have been quite difficult as a parent.

But Kim found it stressful to examine her previous parenting practices, which she described as inadequate and ill informed. The women believed that even though analysing at a deeper level could be problematic, it resulted in their parenting style changing for the better. Angelina, like Kim, now over-analysed her parenting decisions but this critical approach brought benefits to her parenting:

> I criticized myself heavily as a parent … each module that we have done has made me think about my own parenting.
>
> (Angelina)

> I think that's more about finding out things about yourself as a person that perhaps you weren't in a position to know … I think that's what it's helped me to see, there are lots of things that I could have done or there are lots of things that might have been there to support me but they weren't there at the time and I didn't know any of those things … if that [being a single mum] was now I think I would have been able to deal with it better and I would have had more of an understanding of what my children needed and a better grasp of myself maybe to hold it together for them a bit better.
>
> (Kim)

As women change their perspectives and parenting style it is natural that those around notice. Partners and family members are often the first to notice the positive impact on the family:

> She's learning some great stuff to actually bring back home … having more knowledge about certain areas certainly helps you deal with behaviour management.
>
> (Bradley)

> My Mum and Dad think that I've become very, hhmmm, a lot more patient as a mother and more interested in explaining to my children and getting them to sort of think about things for themselves rather than possibly how I used to parent which was like, 'No, because I've said so and that's enough of it', sort of thing you know, 'I've told you why, it's just that's it'.
>
> (Angelina)

As we have seen, transformation through increasing knowledge changes parenting behaviour and identity as a mother. In Marie's case, she was very protective of her children and 'wrapped them up in cotton wool'.

She had lacked self-belief and self-esteem, and believed this restricted the opportunities she gave her children. She feared the risks of horse riding or climbing trees. Through her studies, she realized the importance of creating opportunities for her children to make decisions and become independent. Marie's self-transformation completely changed her ideas on parenting:

> The course has completely changed me as a parent ... My children have a completely different childhood now ... I always said, 'You can't ride [horse ride]', because there was a panic at her [daughter] hurting herself, she is now riding, she's just spending more time outside ... My children have a completely different childhood now, it has just fundamental, how much can one parent change in nine months?

Through increased knowledge and changing parenting practices, women become better educational role models for their children:

> This will make me a good strong positive role model for them ... I want them to grow up confident ... the best way to teach your children is by doing it yourself.
>
> (Doris)

> I think they [children] have a bit more confidence in what they could achieve based on me achieving things as well ... I think that their aspirations have been raised as well and I'd like to think that if I had a degree then there is more chance that they will go further in education.
>
> (Kim)

The women's increasing confidence also affected how others viewed them. For example, Marie's daughter Katie (aged 14) commented on how her mother had changed during the course and revealed how she felt about her mother and stepfather's disintegrating relationship during Marie's studies:

> Mummy has become a lot stronger since she's been doing the course, she's become a better parent all round, its put Harry [stepfather] to the test as it's shown how much he does/doesn't care about how Mummy feels about what she wants to do. I look up to Mummy a lot more, she's become a lot more of an inspiration.
>
> (Katie, Marie's daughter)

These two examples demonstrate how HE study can effect a change in knowledge and perspectives that positively enhances parenting.

Conflict between being a mother and being a student

However, the contrasting roles of mother and student can create conflict:

> ... but Sunday afternoon it was sort of I felt like I needed to do something, give some time to him [partner] and to the children because I think he needs me to ... I do feel guilty because although I'm in the house I'm not really there and I have to not ignore, well, I don't know if ignore is the right word, I feel guilty when I know that they are either sat at home not doing anything fun because I'm studying or they've gone out to do something fun and I'm not with them. So I do feel guilty but it's weighing it up I suppose.
>
> (Kim)

As Kim found, feeling pulled between motherhood and student work can be really difficult to manage. Finding time to study (particularly when assignment deadlines are looming) is difficult, so women make compromises or behave in ways that make them uncomfortable:

> At the weekend, with the children, he [partner] will take them out, I feel terrible because I can't go, but the kids seem to have a great time, and they don't seem to worry. They don't seem to think Mummy is not here, umm, coz they don't come across in that way at all. I think I have just learned that's how it is now sometimes ... It has been really hard, and I have felt guilty about things, you know, not being able to do more with the kids. There have been times when I have not been able to go to sports day events, or nativities ... that has been really difficult and it must have been difficult on them as well.
>
> (Heidi)

> With the kids, because they saw a very different mum, they saw a very stressed mum in those times and I was crying a lot at home ... and in those first two assignments I think they saw a very different mum ... it was tough, the kids would just go, 'It's assignment time again' ... It's just that you want to be there for them and it's just that I felt very guilty ... and they were all fine but they would just know that mum would snap a little bit.
>
> (Christina)

HE study demands time *away* from the family, but also affects time *with* the family if women become preoccupied with the course. Both Doris and Kim found it hard not to think about their studies while spending time with their partners:

> I think because it is so demanding, you can't switch your brain off from it can you? You really can't, so even if David [partner] says, 'Let's just leave it [study] for tonight, let's just sit down and watch a film, have a glass of wine, switch off', I'll be watching the film and thinking ohh, my brain is constantly ticking, thinking I need to think about that, and think about this, and I think probably a lot of the time, my mind wasn't really concentrating 100 per cent ... But I cannot switch off from the studying and relax until that assignment is in the file and ready to go.
>
> (Doris)

> I think for him he said that this is harder than if I had a job because I don't switch off from it and it's everywhere. The books are everywhere!
>
> (Kim)

Switching off from study is difficult because the women students become absorbed by thoughts of assignment deadlines and topic content. It takes time to master new ideas and information and students often mull over their assignments for a long time before they start writing. So being unable to switch off from study can create conflict between family life and student life.

Hilary was the only single parent in my research sample, which was centred on couples. But her story was worth including as an alternative example of transformation and resulting conflict. A single parent with no extended family support, Hilary was solely responsible for her children's care and well-being. This meant that she faced pressures and it affected how she prioritized her study time and juggled her obligations:

> I feel more stimulated, generally more aware of looking at things in different ways. I adjust how I do things in my own routines ... It is not a negative, but I have tussles but largely with myself and what I can achieve. I will not give up on the children so have to relinquish study time and achievement ... I have a lot of frustration, as I do not give the foundation degree 100 per cent, but feel I am giving what I can. I could give more but what gives? ... It does work, as long as I am happy to under-achieve ... I won't compromise!

Hilary recognized that her thinking was transformed but saw limits to how much time she could devote to her studies when she didn't want to change her role as a mum. There was no one to whom she could delegate some of her mothering duties and responsibilities. Hilary didn't wish to put study time ahead of family time, so decided to limit the amount of time she studied, rather than compromising her time with her children.

To sum up: when women begin HE, they actively decide how much to put their own career needs and personal development above the needs of the family. They worry about how their studies will affect their children as their role as a mother often comes first. When women students begin to change their parenting practices or their beliefs about being a mother, conflict can arise, mainly in the form of their own internal battle and feelings of guilt. Some find this conflict hard to handle but by focusing on the long-term benefits of their study – to themselves and their family – they feel able to justify becoming a mum who is also a student.

Strategies to support your changing identity and being both mum and HE student

Changing your identity is an aspect of starting HE that is to be expected. The following strategies may help you to manage these self-transformations:

- Be aware that your approaches to mothering and parenting may well change. How will you support your family and how will they support you in these changes?
- Accept that this is the pathway you have chosen – try not to be overwhelmed by feelings of guilt over your changing roles or identity as a mother.
- Consider getting support, if you can, with aspects of your new and demanding daily routine, or devise strategies to reorder your priorities: what are essential tasks, what are desirable, what are not needed?
- Try to plan your study time so that you can take time out for social activities without feeling preoccupied (see Chapter 7 for more on this).
- If you still feel preoccupied during family time, have a notebook to hand to write down your 'lightbulb moments' then leave them and focus on the family again.
- Try to remodel your identity as a mother who studies. Consider the long-term benefits to yourself and your family to help you position yourself more positively and feel less guilty.

Chapter 4

Changing concepts of self

I will not give up on the course and chose that over my marriage
... I have a changed perspective ... I own my own space ... I am
in charge of me.

(Marie)

Students begin an HE course because they want to change something
about themselves, whether it is to enhance their knowledge or their career
opportunities. HE transforms ways of thinking and ways of behaving for
women (Edwards, 1993a; Merrill, 1999; Parr, 2000; Pascall and Cox, 1993).

A change to your self-image is to be expected as you grapple with
your increasing knowledge base and changed viewpoints. It is important
to be aware of this before you start and during your study. A change of
self-image can affect all areas of life, enhancing self-confidence, changing
perspectives, working life and conversations.

Self-image

Self-image is about how we see ourselves and is built up over time. Sometimes
experiences at school can leave women with little confidence in their own
educational abilities. A gap in education can also diminish their view of
their academic capabilities (Webber, 2014). Negative experiences at school
and a lack of self-confidence can then form a barrier to further study:

> I was much less confident than what I am now, umm, I always felt
> that I wasn't as good as other people ... I thought I would never
> amount to anything educationally.
>
> (Doris)

> Right from the start, education became an issue. It was a shame
> really and when I went to secondary school it was the same
> thing again. I don't feel they picked up on things [educational
> difficulties] enough and offered you that support that I needed at
> that time, since then because of that, or perhaps I think it's the
> teenage years; I think I rebelled a bit.
>
> (Heidi)

> I struggled, I really found school hard … because I hated school, I
> struggled with school … but somewhere deep inside of me I knew
> that I wanted more.
>
> (Esme)

Such feelings are affected by how we are labelled by others educationally or
by a position we assume. For example, Heidi and Esme had been labelled as
low achievers by their school teachers, whereas Doris had labelled herself
as not being good enough even though her teachers encouraged her to go
on to HE.

However, confidence can develop from studying at HE level.
For example:

> As time has gone by the confidence I have has grown and also
> the achievement that I never had at school though I could, you
> know I didn't do badly at school, I got you know full O levels but
> knowing certain comments that the teachers had made and I've
> thought I've got to do this for myself.
>
> (Christina)

> I didn't have confidence in myself; I didn't have confidence in my
> ability to do this when I first started. I do feel a bit more confident
> in myself … I don't know actually. I think I'm pleased I've been
> able to do what I have done, I didn't think I'd be able to get as
> good a mark as I have done.
>
> (Jennifer)

Having a break in study can also make women apprehensive about returning
to education (Webber, 2014). By identifying their personal motivations for
studying, women can push on to achieve their end goals:

> I have always wanted to have a degree and actually doing it for
> yourself is the most important thing … I think you have to want
> to do it for you, not because you are pressured into doing it …
> otherwise you haven't got the heart, the heart's not there.
>
> (Christina)

Self-esteem is also important. Marie had had difficulties in her marriage
before she returned to study. She related how destructive relationships had
affected her self-esteem in the past and described losing her self-confidence,
self-control, self-belief and self-respect. These relationships had not
acknowledged her achievements or nurtured her self-esteem. Marie's current
partner wanted her to achieve status through a career rather than being a

stay-at-home mother. This caused her to doubt her abilities in making her own choices:

> So my self-respect and self-esteem at this point were very low ... I was pretty reliant on people that weren't very good for me ... he [partner] consistently said, 'You have to do more, being a mum is not enough': he did not respect the mother's role.

For women like Heidi, Doris, Esme, Christina, Jennifer and Marie, who had suffered from low self-confidence, entering HE study can be challenging and create uncertainty. But the women were able to put this aside, believing that HE offered them a different life. Marie was looking for a change in direction; she wanted a purposeful career and to succeed at something by herself. Betty had previously found status through her paid work but felt this was lost when she became a mother. Betty saw HE as a space to reconstruct her identity and regain respect and status. A change in self-image occurred as their perceptions about themselves were transformed. A period of unrest should be expected, as women and their families adapt to the woman's changed identity.

Increased knowledge

Through HE studies, women's perspectives change as their knowledge accrues (Cherrington and Thornton, 2013). In turn, women's values base and beliefs change. They begin to understand topics and situations through reflective and analytical thought (Lehrer, 2013; Thompson and Thompson, 2008). Through education, women become more reflective and look at things differently (Osgood, 2006).

Developing reflective skills through academic study then influences many areas of a woman's life. In the case of my participants, reflection occurred around issues of child development and learning, as well as their relationships. Learning, reflection and change are not limited to the area of study, but affect other areas too: a woman's role as mother, partner, wife, friend or worker. You should be aware that your attitudes and perspectives may change in many aspects of your life and conversations may change accordingly. As Mercer notes, the 'academic and personal can be interlinked' (Mercer, 2007: 24). One student's partner observed:

> It does make her think twice about how she interacts with her children ... I think she is more reflective, yeah, because I think it is easy as you get older to get tunnel vision and I think it has opened her mind to new ways and means.

(Alan)

Therefore, it is helpful to warn family members, before you start HE, that your perspectives may change during your study. Some family members expect everything to stay the same, but this is unlikely:

> David [partner] has seen me change, and he has really struggled with this kind of confident person now who doesn't just sit quietly and say nothing. To him that was quite difficult, umm, but I think he has pretty much come to terms with it, because he wasn't able to initially, and that has only been recent.
>
> (Doris)

Changes in perspective can transform identity in a number of ways:

> I no longer take things personally.
>
> (Doris)

> I look at the bigger picture now ... I look at things differently now ... my perceptions are broader than before.
>
> (Esme)

> I am less erratic now.
>
> (Kim)

> It has given me more of a presence now, I always over-simplified things before, now I don't need to.
>
> (Maggie)

Increased knowledge and a fresh perspective can bring about fundamental changes in other areas of a woman's life, such as parenting (see Chapter 3), friendships and work. This in turn affects her self-confidence.

'The more you achieve, the more you think you can do this'

A number of studies have shown that women gain self-confidence when they are HE students (see Mercer, 2007; Christie *et al.*, 2008), because the HE environment is seen as a safe and supportive space where self-confidence can be developed (Mezirow, 1978).

Self-confidence is enhanced when women achieve in their studies, although they may find assessments harder to cope with when they have been out of education for a time (Bowl, 2003). Passing assignments lifts their self-confidence:

> My grades were getting okay and that was certainly helping my confidence ... my confidence has definitely grown on the course because I am doing it.
>
> (Angelina)

> I do now feel that I am ready to take on things I never thought I would be able to ... I feel much more confident in making decisions.
>
> (Doris)

As women develop a sense of confidence in their ability and learn to trust their instincts, they begin to see themselves differently:

> I have become more confident in my own capabilities once I did those first two assignments ... after repeatedly getting passes, you then think, well actually what I am putting in I know, it's just having faith in yourself and what has happened as the years have gone on, my identity is thinking well, actually I do know what I am talking about ... It is just having that confidence in yourself and I think each time you get a grade ... you feel better about yourself.
>
> (Christina)

As her self-confidence developed, Doris's relationships with her partner and her family changed. She felt more able to have discussions with her father-in-law, whose job had always intimidated her. Doris realized that she was now more knowledgeable and able than before:

> He is very well read and very intelligent and even though I got on really well with him, he is a lovely man, I feel a little bit more equal with him now, I don't feel quite so, what is the word I am looking for, I don't mean insignificant, I just felt inferior ... I do feel that as I have done this I have proved something to myself, which is something that is important, something I had to do. I feel that I can hold my head up a little bit more now and say, 'Actually, I am okay, don't look down your nose at me as I am doing alright.' And that is important, that is really important.

Most of the women saw confidence as an aspect of their changed identity. As their perceptions of themselves and their self-confidence strengthened, so did their aspirations. Increased self-assurance can make women students consider possibilities for themselves that they had not entertained before:

> I think the biggest thing is, I do now feel that I am ready to take on things that I thought I would never be able to. Even silly things, and you know, if someone had said 10 years ago that you will be doing a degree, eventually you'll be travelling out of area to study I would think, 'No I wouldn't go out of my town', or whatever … and actually, I am ready to do that, whereas before I just thought I cannot do that, I don't you know? … I feel ready to branch out and I'm confident to do that.
>
> (Doris)

Increased confidence at work

Increasing self-confidence has an impact on a woman's self-esteem, self-belief and family relationships but it can also affect their work skills, capabilities and relationships. This can come as a surprise for women students and their colleagues. Greater self-confidence can positively affect team dynamics within a work situation:

> I feel more confident with having those conversations with staff, with leading a staff meeting but also understanding them now … The confidence is the biggest one at the moment; it is my confidence in knowing … I don't know whether it is because I'm confident, but that they're [colleagues] asking me my opinion more.
>
> (Christina)

> But I sort of feel that other professionals will now ask for my opinions, views, thoughts on individual children and situations and as a result of that I think that means that relationships have been strengthened … because I feel that my views are now much more respected which is more inclusive isn't it?
>
> (Doris)

> I know that I am capable now, whereas before I was doing it and everybody [at work] was telling me that I was doing a good job but I wasn't quite sure if they were encouraging me because I needed it, now I know that actually I know, it sounds big headed but I can do it … Well, at work it's made me more confident with all of my colleagues.
>
> (Maggie)

However, becoming more confident in their abilities can cause conflict in the workplace when women alter their working approaches in line with their new knowledge. Some colleagues might feel intimidated by the transformations they see:

> I am more confident in my own instincts if that makes sense, ... but that can be hard, because I work as a learning support assistant, I'm not a higher-level teaching assistant, I am not a teacher, I am a learning support assistant alongside of other learning support assistants. Some of them are level 2, some of them are just studying towards level 3, but because I am now just finishing my level 5, you can get that clash ... I think they think that I think that I am better than them, I certainly don't. I'm in there to muck in and get on with it with everyone else. But there are times and I might make decisions or do things that perhaps they might not ... I think I am more confident to do that, and I know that I can do that but yes, that can be difficult.
>
> (Doris)

Yet some women feel unable to commit 100 per cent to every aspect of their lives, and it can be their work that gets neglected:

> I started to feel guilty because I wasn't there for the staff, especially in the first and second year of my foundation degree. There were periods in those academic years that I hit an all-time low and luckily I had the staff to go phewwwwwe (*gestured being scooped up*).
>
> (Christina)

> So the only focus was my college work ... I think even work suffered, I think I even lost the enthusiasm I had to work with the families [family support worker]. Working with families has always been a passion for me, I felt I sort of just did it, I don't think I gave them a good service like I usually do, so that I know in those areas yes definitely I think it affected me.
>
> (Esme)

Although some women feel that they are treated less well at work because of their HE transformations, others found their status raised:

> I think people do relate to you differently when they know that you have been studying, so there are people that I work alongside of, from other agencies [Doris works with children] who will have different conversations now than they would have a few years ago ... I think the conversations now are more professional,

> not just what I observe but also what do I think, what do I think about this child? These are very professional people with lots of experience so that's a nice compliment for somebody to say, 'Well what do you think?', because that probably wouldn't have happened before. I now feel more professional, I feel that this is acknowledged by other professionals and I think that kind of ties in with that because I feel more confident, I act more confident.
>
> (Doris)

Identity change is a key consequence of studying at HE level for women. Through their increased knowledge, their perspectives change, possibly affecting both home life and working life. Even the women's topics of conversations change as their viewpoints alter. As women take on new challenges, their personal beliefs are challenged and changed through the process of reflection. Working life is transformed as women act more confidently, thus impinging on team dynamics and relationships.

In short, knowledge gained through HE affects all aspects of a woman's life. Although women welcome their development of knowledge, self-belief and confidence, those around them sometimes struggle.

Strategies to support changing self-image

The followings strategies may help you and your family adjust to the new you:

- If you are concerned about starting HE because you have had difficulties with learning in the past, take steps to develop your study skills. Don't be afraid to ask for help, take advice about your work and use feedback to develop your writing skills.
- Be aware that you may have chosen your course because of a wish to change something about yourself – others may not be prepared for such changes.
- Discuss with those around you your motivations for completing the course; this will help them to accept the new you.
- Increasing confidence can affect your working relationships; be prepared for this and be sensitive that colleagues may need time to adjust.
- Do be aware that sometimes HE can be a roller-coaster of highs and lows. As well as increasing, your self-confidence can take a dip at times as you adjust to juggling HE and family life. This is to be expected!
- Use your HE peer group as a sounding board to discuss the effects of your transforming perspectives on family and work life. You may find that they are going through similar experiences.

Part Three

The impact on relationships

My position in the family has changed massively to one of respect and strength, I've never had that in my family.

(Esme)

Part Two explored the ways in which studying powerfully affects a woman's identity and confidence. As her knowledge base increases, her self-image, self-esteem and the ways she views the world all change. A change in perspective affects her parenting style and beliefs about motherhood. Women feel more self-assured in their relationships with others within the family and at work. Part Three explores how being a woman who studies can affect relationships with partners, children, parents and friends.

Chapter 5
'It's changed everyone's life'

It's changed both our lives; it's changed everyone's life, even the kids!

(Alan)

Actually the biggest change is in my relationship, that's the impact.

(Esme)

When women study, there are practical implications for the family. Family routines and structures change. This affects the woman's position in the family and their relationship with their partner and children.

Impact on partners

HE changes relationships between women and their partners, transforming roles in three possible ways. First, as the woman's identity changes and she becomes more self-assured, this is likely to affect her partner. This in turn can change the relationship, for example their conversations, as the woman develops different viewpoints and new interests. Finally, the different roles within the relationship can change as it adjusts.

Partners notice the changes in the women as they develop self-reflective approaches and begin to see things from different perspectives:

The educational side has given her the belief in herself perhaps a bit more.

(Bradley)

The women saw themselves as calmer, more analytical, more confident and content. For some, this was positive and enhanced their relationship with their partner as communication improved. Angelina commented:

I think it is the fact that he's [partner] accepted that this [analytical approach] is now part of me.

Yet Bradley did not accept Angelina's new approach straight away. Initially, there was a period of friction as he struggled to cope with the change:

This caused quite a lot of conflict between me and my husband in the first year because something would happen [with the

> children] and I would say, 'Hold on a minute, let's have a think about this, why is he [son] doing this?' ... That kind of analytical approach really wound him [partner] up ... I think he adapted to what I was becoming and things I was saying and I think I probably toned it down a bit ... a lot of the conflict we had in year one has gone.
>
> (Angelina)

It is interesting that Angelina 'toned down' her approach and viewpoints when she felt that they were causing conflict. Women use this strategy to strike a balance between expressing their changing viewpoints and ensuring that family members are accepting of them. This compromise worked for Angelina; by her second year of study the conflict was resolved.

On the other hand, Ross enjoyed having an increasingly confident partner in Maggie, as he saw her HE as a positive experience: with confidence she became more content and fulfilled:

> I think she's more self-satisfied and confident in herself because it's you know, the satisfaction of being able to do that as a mature student has sort of increased her overall confidence ... I'm pleased she's doing it really, it's helping her to be more open-minded about things.
>
> (Ross)

Not all men welcomed a change in their partner, but those who didn't were in the minority:

> It has been really tricky. David has seen me change, and he has really struggled with this kind of confident person now who just doesn't sit quietly and say nothing ... he doesn't have to cocoon me and protect me as much.
>
> (Doris)

Eighty per cent of the women studied emphasized the positive effects that their HE was having on their relationship, although my study showed that both partners need time to get used to the new situation. Both partners found that their more analytical and reflective discussions were more rewarding and it was easier for any issues to be resolved:

> We do discuss things now and we maybe over-analyse things together because Matt [partner] tends to do that as well.
>
> (Kim)

> The main major difference has been in my marriage, in the last year I do feel that my husband and I have grown a lot closer.
>
> (Angelina)

Not all the women felt closer to their partner. From the start, Doris saw her study as causing their relationship to suffer and it was under strain during most of her course:

> It's an adjustment. And it has been really difficult, and I felt for a long time that he [partner] really resented me doing the degree, which he now says it wasn't that. You know we had a real big talk about it a couple of weeks ago, and he said, 'I'm really, really proud of you, I see how hard you work, but that is just so difficult and we are trying to do so much, and the more we try to do, the less we have together' … I do also think there is a little element as well of jealousy there as he hasn't done it, and David has pretty much done everything, this is something he hasn't done. So he is not able to, I think he almost feels that he can't join in, he can't sit down and say, he can't share with me even though I want to share with him as he hasn't done it. I don't know if he feels jealous as he hasn't done it, therefore my wife will be more academic than me, I don't think it's that, it's just that he can't share it with me … I felt it had really separated us, which I think it almost did, but I think we've managed to put it back … It has been really difficult, really difficult.

Doris's story highlights several significant issues. Her partner resented her participating in HE. Firstly, this was because he appeared to feel 'left out' and 'isolated'. The women have new experiences, making new friends, being in a different environment and learning new things. Secondly, when women create study time, either at university or in the home, this leaves less time for their partner. Finally, Doris felt that her partner possibly resented her HE studies because it made him feel 'less academic'. Partners may feel 'left behind' and that they are at a different level academically. This is compounded by the woman's developing perspective and the changed nature and quality of her conversations.

Even though Doris thought her partner resented her studies, they were able to resolve the conflict when she approached the end of the course. She believed that her relationship was strengthened through the resolution of their difficulties, and this helped Doris justify her learning:

> Although my studies are respected [by her partner] they are not always welcomed … and the impact on relationships, well it has caused issues but actually the flip side of that, you know the issues have to be resolved so every time you resolve an issue you are strengthening something.
>
> (Doris)

There were also tensions over renegotiating childcare or household tasks, highlighting or exacerbating underlying friction:

> I think though that if there is anything there, any areas of strain that they will be highlighted …Through the pressures that come about at some point, to different degrees you know.
>
> (Maggie)

The women were so heavily focused on their studies and on ensuring that the children did not miss out that they usually sacrificed time with their partners:

> Joe [partner] probably was not a huge priority either at those points: all that really was important was that the children were okay and that I could get on with my studies. I did what I had to do … He understands what pressure I am under and he doesn't seem to mind.
>
> (Heidi)

Eighty per cent of the couples were able to cope with having less time for each other as they seemed to accept that this was only for a fixed period of time. When they had a strong relationship at the start, the couples felt this finite period of unrest could be managed:

> You need a strong foundation and you both possibly need to have that initial agreement of this is the journey you are about to go on, this is where you want to be, I think you need to have that quite clear and both be bought into the idea and ethos of it to be honest.
>
> (Bradley)

> I think because, because I let go of these things and I had to say to myself you can't do it all, you know let go of that, concentrate on that, and then once you know where you are with your college work you can work on your relationship, you know, you are only letting that go for a little while.
>
> (Esme)

These stories show two different ways that couples manage less time for each other. Bradley and Angelina discussed the importance of Angelina's course for her career progression, which would bring long-term financial gains for the whole family. This helped Bradley to see that it was worth making sacrifices. Esme's approach is quite different. She felt unable to cope with both HE study and relationship conflict, so decided just to focus on her HE studies, choosing to put her relationship on hold. This strategy gave her breathing space, and it was proved successful because of the strength of their relationship and their both agreeing to invest in their relationship later.

Christina's approach was an extension of Esme's. She recognized that at times she needed to prioritize her studies over her family but developed a strategy of weekend family time and 'date' time with her partner which seemed to suit the needs of everyone:

> We would have time when they [children] were younger on a Saturday and Sunday because I always said, even up to the last hand-in date on the following week, Saturday would be family day. Even most recently in the last few years. It would be Dominic [partner] and I's day and we would go out to lunch. Saturday was a 'lunch date'. That's what we kept and I think that's what we had to keep, definitely as a husband and wife we had to keep that … actually those Saturdays were precious because we caught up and we talked about the kids and we just spent most of Saturday in town, just talking really and I think that was really important … I don't know I think he [partner] would have coped without this but I think the strain would've been there … I think he would have struggled, because he wasn't speaking you know, and he needs to offload sometimes and I think those Saturdays became his offload, just talking, definitely.

What is interesting here is Christina's awareness of the effect on her partner of spending less time together. So they created a weekly 'date' day – which also gave Christina valuable time away from her studies, helping her to avoid burn-out.

But it is difficult to avoid stress altogether. All of the women suffered from some degree of stress while on the HE programme and this sometimes affected their partner. Increased stress led to difficulties in a number of ways: through the woman becoming tired, grumpy or distancing herself from the family; through the partner having to take on more responsibilities; and through friction and tension when assignments were due in. Assignment deadlines caused additional friction as meeting deadlines was difficult when the women were juggling so many responsibilities.

Kim described the financial stress and pressure on the relationship caused by studying rather than working, but believed the rewards compensated:

> He [partner] worries about finances and although our finances are fine and we have the student loan, you don't just get the student loan do you? There is so much paperwork which he deals with … he feels that the rewards are worth it, that we have invested so much time and money and just our whole, and not just me …

But her partner found the additional pressure of supporting her – financially, emotionally and practically – led to unexpected health issues:

> He has had to do all the picking up [children from school] and it's really affected his stress levels and because there is less time … he didn't think our relationship was affected although it was impacted by the sort of ricochet of the stress in the day to day. For him he said that it magnifies the stress because things that I might have been doing before if I'm not doing them they still have to be done … last week he started taking beta blockers for stress and anxiety, it's just the length of time that you can manage.

Acknowledging stress and putting strategies in place is important. You may need to access support from your tutor, peer group or a healthcare professional.

Although stress increased at assignment deadlines, the men viewed their partners with a certain amount of pride. As HE transformed the women's identities, it also changed how their partners saw them:

> It makes her [Esme] go up in my estimations a little bit because it is hard and you know I am all for further education and stuff.
>
> (Alan)

> I'm very proud of her [Angelina] and what she has done.
>
> (Bradley)

This affected how the women were positioned by their partners in the relationship. Before starting HE, 40 per cent of the women described not feeling equal to their partners. Their negative early educational experiences may have left them with little self-confidence in their own abilities (see Chapter 4). Once in HE, the women felt they could be more informed and analytical in discussions. As new possible career options opened out, they felt they had higher standing and status with their partner. These shifts certainly enhanced Kim's relationship, as discussions with her partner became more interesting:

> I think doing the course has actually enriched our relationship because maybe it's brought me up to the same sort of I don't know if it's the same level but you know we have lots of discussions and things and I think that makes it more interesting.
>
> (Kim)

The relationships were also affected by the change in division of labour in the household, as 80 per cent of the men took on a greater share of childcare, even looking after the children at weekends to facilitate additional study time:

> My husband does have to do slightly more ... when they [children] are sick and I have a college day, I have made him do it.
>
> (Jennifer)

Eighty per cent of the women also relied on their partner to take a greater share in housework, generally with cooking or cleaning. This gave the women more time to devote to their studies, making day-to-day life more manageable:

> Ross [partner] has definitely helped on a practical level ... His role has changed at home ... he's changed to adapt to the changing needs of the household.
>
> (Maggie)

> There has been a bit of a role change, I do a bit more around the house than I did, although I did do a bit, I probably find myself doing more now.
>
> (Alan)

The identity strands of mother and student

How women handle identity change, times of tension or a change within their relationship can be linked to separating or connecting the different aspects of their lives as mother, partner and student (Edwards, 1993a). Some of the women tried to *connect* the different aspects of their identity and merge being mother and wife with being an HE student. They were quite open about their study and talked about it at home. Some women involved their children in their studies, bringing them into the university to show them where they were studying. This helped the children to connect to their mum's studies and to feel part of it instead of resenting the diminished attention. These women saw themselves holistically and couldn't *separate* aspects of their identity. Others kept the different aspects of their identity separate and hid their study as a bid to survive as a student, trying to keep the identities of student, mother and partner distinct.

Some women felt it important to share the journey together and connect the HE study with their relationship with their partner. The students often use the metaphor of a journey to describe the highs and lows of their HE experiences and the sense of an ultimate destination. Sharing the journey meant involving their family in their study, discussing topics, proofreading, studying in the midst of family activities and talking to the children about their career goals. For others (like Doris), separating their HE study and their relationship with their partner was necessary in order to maintain the relationship and reduce conflict.

Kim, Angelina and Esme all discussed their studies and involved their partners in proofreading their work. Through connecting their studies with their partner in these ways, the women were able to merge the boundaries between HE study and family life and to gain support and encouragement:

> He reads all my work that I do, he proofreads everything that I do.
>
> (Kim)

> I think for me, the turning point was probably, do you continue going on like this [stress in relationship because of HE] or do you talk and get it over and done with and say listen if this is what's going to happen then this is what I need of support from you because if we are going to go down this road [HE] you need to be with me on this journey, or it [relationship] will come to an end.
>
> (Esme)

Jennifer neither actively discussed her studies with her partner nor concealed them, yet having his permission and approval to study was important to her. As well as his help with childcare and household tasks, she also wanted her studies to be valued and confirmed for the ways it changed her identity:

> He said, 'I am happy for you to do it but I want to see that it goes somewhere'. I see what he means, basically he means that, 'You are putting this much time and effort into it, I want to know that you are going to earn more money at the end', ... whereas I wanted him to say, 'I want you to do it because you want to do it and it's good for you', but that's not quite what I got.
>
> (Jennifer)

This response is not uncommon, although Jennifer found it frustrating. Many partners (and sometimes parents) measure study in terms of financial gain rather than self-fulfilment.

Doris felt that she was given no choice but to separate her HE studies from her partner in order to maintain her relationship. But she did not feel it necessary to hide her studies from her children and she actively shared them with her children and enjoyed the encouragement and support. She presumed that her partner felt threatened by her changed identity and her studies as he offered little support and at times withdrew it completely – an unspoken sign that he was unhappy with her decision to enter HE:

> I would say there have been times where he [partner] has done less, almost to dig his heels in to prove a point.
>
> (Doris)

But her partner's lack of support proved to be a motivating factor for Doris. Although it upset her, she became more determined to complete the course and achieve success. Sometimes when women face opposition to their studies, as Doris did, they become even more determined to succeed, to prove that there are benefits to studying or to justify the conflict their study incurred:

> This [HE] is something that I want and it was just sheer determination … So you find ways of doing it without causing too many ripples … I haven't got the energy for anything petty anymore so it's just easier to shrug your shoulders and say, 'Hey, ho!', and walk away from it [argument with partner over HE study] … As soon as you hand in that last assignment … as soon as all of that pressure is now off I thought I can go and talk to David [partner] without worrying, with a clear head.
>
> (Doris)

> I think I internalized the stress and I thought you know what, I'm just going to go with the flow, I just don't have no puff left to fight. So the only focus was my college work … I think I had to let go of those things before I could find me …
>
> (Esme)

Connecting or separating the different aspects of their identity depended on the nature of their relationship, their assessment workload and their partner's acceptance or rejection of their studies, rather than being a conscious choice. This situation changed over the course of their studies.

The women who separated their studies from their partner found it more problematic in the long run – trying to keep their identity as a mother, partner and HE student separate was at best playing for time. Resolving the conflict at some point appeared to be essential even if, as in Marie's case, the resolution was a permanent separation.

The women hid their studies either from their children to prevent them from feeling left out or neglected, or they chose to hide their studies from their partner to reduce conflict. Blurring the edges between the roles of mother, partner and student seemed to be an effective strategy for some, who adopted strategies of separating or connecting their studies with the family as appropriate.

'My children have a completely different childhood now'

Being a mum remained the most important part of the women's identities; how their HE study affected their children concerned them greatly. They worried about the potentially negative impact of studying on their children's well-being.

Accordingly, some mothers tried to study when their children were not around. The women told their children about their studies but tried to keep the times their children saw them studying to a minimum, not to avoid resentment or conflict but so the children would not feel neglected or think that their mother's studies were more important to her than they were.

The women tried to reduce their feelings of guilt over studying by justifying the way that they felt their HE study had benefited their children and the whole family. They identified three main areas of benefit. One was the change in parenting style (see Chapter 3) that resulted from their newly acquired knowledge and consequent change of perspective. The second impact was the way it could influence the children's education. Finally, the children's relationships with their fathers were enriched because they spent more time together.

Benefits for the children's education

Thanks to the women's greater knowledge and self-confidence, and their new status, they felt more able to influence their children's education for the better. Jennifer used her confidence and new knowledge about children's development to fight for her daughter at primary school:

> I think it's having an impact on them [children] ... as I have been fighting a transitional battle ... I'm fighting for better working between reception class and pre-school, because they are so much

younger going in now ... I have the knowledge to say actually
this is best for the children and we are doing it.

(Jennifer)

HE gave women the skills, wider perspective and confidence in their own
abilities. They saw education differently and applied their belief in the value
of education to their children. Kim, Doris, Jennifer, Maggie and Angelina all
believe that through their HE studies they have been effective educational
role models for their children and raised their own and their children's
educational aspirations. Because of their own achievements, the children
believed they too could achieve more:

I want them both to study as highly as they can as early as
they can.

(Doris)

My expectations have changed ... their [children] aspirations
and my aspirations have changed and the goal posts have moved
quite far from perhaps what it was before I started the course ...
but I think they have a bit more confidence in what they could
achieve based on me achieving things as well and because, I don't
know whether it was just something I hadn't really considered
before or I thought oh they just go to school and they will learn
there but when I do things there is a bit more focus on what they
are doing and I think that their aspirations have been raised as
well and I'd like to think that if I had a degree then there is more
chance that they will go further in education.

(Kim)

Although they felt 'time poor' (Edwards, 1993a), because they had to
manage their daily routines effectively they were able to prioritize what
they considered the most important aspects of being a 'good mother'.
They now saw the importance of parental involvement in their child's
education and educational support at home. They began emphasizing the
importance of reading, offering more focused support with homework and
asking the children challenging questions. Mother and child relationships
were enhanced, as older children offered support with educational study
(see Chapter 8). The relationship between the mothers, their children and
education became a more important focus than before:

I'm far more aware of every single thing ... reading with them, and everything really, just little things I am far more aware of things.

(Heidi)

I think homework wise it has had an impact on her [daughter] ... it's positive; they can see that actually you have got to sit down and work.

(Jennifer)

For women like Doris, whose partner may have felt intimidated by HE, increasing the value of education at home could cause additional strain on their relationship. Prioritizing education may not be a goal that your partner shares. Being aware of areas of conflict and difference is important in overcoming tension.

The children in many of the families in my study became more independent and less reliant on their mothers. Although the women tried to minimize the amount of time they studied in front of the children, there were times when they had to deal with an exceptionally high workload. When their mums were busy with study, the older children assisted the younger ones, bringing the siblings closer. Children developed problem-solving skills to resolve sibling disputes and take more responsibility for themselves:

I think their [children] coping strategies were they learnt to cook *(laughs)*, you know they became very independent.

(Christina)

Developing positive educational outcomes for children and adapting to their mother studying are findings that have already been discussed in other studies and continue to be the case here (Edwards, 1993a; Edwards 1993b; Merrill, 1999). A new finding from my study is the effect of the women's studies on the relationship between the children and their father. It is this factor that I wish to focus more fully on.

Relationships between fathers and children

During the course of the women's HE studies, many of the children's relationships with their fathers were transformed as their fathers spent more free time with their children, changed interactions and transformed their own parenting styles.

Before commencing HE, the women were the main carers for their children and saw themselves as being the parent who was emotionally available and accessible to their children. Parenting was not equally weighted and shared between the couple. The women in my study had chosen to work part time so that they could fulfil their expected role as mothers. It is unclear whether their partners or wider social expectations had any influence on this choice. During the course of the HE programme, roles in childcare altered for many of the families:

> They [children] all know that I am busy now and not available all of the time and not expected to be there for everybody all of the time, whereas it was always mum, whatever time, and they know now that it's not always me but it's dad and that's got to be equally acceptable because he is perfectly capable and willing.
>
> (Maggie)

Clearly, Maggie's view of her role as a mother has shifted from before she began her HE study:

> It's kind of like I do whatever is needed for my kids.

Christina and Betty's accounts also show how their roles and their perspectives on what it is to be a mother and father have changed:

> As a mother I ran around after my children, like you do … It's actually been sometimes [during HE] where Dominic [partner] had to take over and I think he's quite enjoyed it. They [children] have always had a good relationship with their dad but I think they have almost benefited more, definitely … I think he has changed in thinking further ahead.
>
> (Christina)

> It's me that's been the one to sort everything out, so it's up to me to kind of organize everyone [before HE]. When Lloyd [partner] started spending more time with the children they wanted to … be with him more and they were happy … really positive for the relationship, definitely.
>
> (Betty)

The children's fathers were called upon to provide more practical and emotional support. Who was responsible for what had to be negotiated between the couple:

> In year one there was a lot of friction definitely and we were both tussling over who gets time and who has to have the children.
>
> (Angelina)

My husband has taken over, he's upped the game and he almost is thinking about it more because he's had to [supporting the children if they have a problem to be resolved], because I haven't always been there and he's been the first point of call so that's worked.

(Christina)

As the fathers planned ahead to provide for their children's needs and enjoyed additional time with them, relationships between the children and their dads were enhanced and transformed. Knowing that the children were receiving emotional and practical support from the fathers and that they were safe and happy did not completely eliminate the women's feelings of guilt; they still felt guilty about not being fully focused on the family:

I do feel guilty as, although I am in the house, I am not really there … I feel guilty when I know that they [children and partner] are either sat at home not doing anything fun because I am working or they've gone out to do something fun and I'm not with them.

(Kim)

As well as feeling guilty about missing out on family time, they felt jealous because their role as a mother seemed to be threatened or taken over. Stepping back from organizing and actively taking part in their children's activities aroused mixed emotions because they wanted to be a certain type of mother but also wanted to achieve well in their studies. To minimize such feelings, some students took HE work with them when they attended children's sporting events. Some with part-time jobs worked fewer hours so they could study while their children were at school, freeing up time for them when they came home. And some just accepted the situation:

When they [children] had football, what I should have done was stay at home and study but they wanted me to watch, so I went and I would read a book, whilst I was waiting in the 15-minute gap.

(Maggie)

I just felt constantly guilty so I dropped some of my hours [paid work] so I could create study time while they were at school.

(Angelina)

At the weekend with the children, yes, he [partner] will take them out, I feel terrible because I can't go, but the kids seem to have a great time and they don't seem to worry ... I think I have just learned that's how it is sometimes ...

(Heidi)

Compromise of this kind is fairly typical. Women students often feel that they never quite get it right and are torn between wanting to be a mum and wanting to be a student and fear neglecting one role when they prioritize the other. Heidi's strategy of trying to accept that 'this is how it is' for a short while seems to work for most. Finding a compromise that suits you and your family will vary from family to family, as discussed later in this chapter.

Transformations to the fathers' parenting

As well as spending more time with their children, the men's parenting changed in response to the women's transformed parenting style:

So it is wearing off on him [partner], what I have learnt ... for example how he would respond to them ... if I am calmer then it would have influenced him, and then he is calmer about things.

(Heidi)

As one father remarked:

Because if she's studied something and she sees the benefits of doing something in a particular way that gets better results, she'd probably talk that through with me ... and then I'd look at that and either agree or disagree and then we'd come to, 'Right, this is our stance on this now together.'

(Bradley)

Kim observed how her partner changed his parenting style after proofreading her work on child development. He attended a parenting course to support his child's behaviour, and his perspective changed as his knowledge grew:

He did a parenting course ... and he was able to understand what they were saying, he was relating it to theories and things he had read in my work, so he was star pupil!

(Kim)

Partners who were supportive emotionally or practically seemed more willing to embrace new ideas in line with their wives' improved knowledge. All of the women who received support from their partner reported a change in his parenting, although the two women who received no support saw no such changes. The men who were open to change in their partners were likewise receptive to change in themselves and family life. Before HE, Doris saw her partner as the dominant and confident one in the relationship, describing herself as a 'mouse'. It is unclear whether her partner's resistance to her HE studies was because of Doris's attempts to change the family's routines to fit around her study or whether it evolved as she became more confident. The discord may have begun while she was considering HE study and actively looking for change.

HE causes profound changes to family relationships through a woman's identity transformation. Relationships with partners can be strengthened when a woman becomes calmer, reflective, analytical and more confident. Discussions become richer and issues are more readily resolved. Some women are granted higher status by their partners so relationships are stronger and more equal. A woman who undertakes HE study can expect changes in her relationship that may prove to be positive or negative.

Some women will experience a period of strain and adjustment if their identity changes are seen negatively by their partner and will use a combination of connecting and separating their studies (Edwards, 1993a). They may enlist their partner's help with proofreading and discuss their studies with him, or they may minimize the effects on their family by hiding their studies. Ultimately, the tensions will need to be resolved, either during the course, as for Marie; or only once the studies are completed, as in Doris's case.

From a mother who studies, children gain new educational role models and an insight into HE. They generally develop greater independence and autonomy and enhance their sibling relationships. Their education can be enhanced through better-informed parents and more parental involvement and the greater valuing of the child's education. When a woman transforms her parenting in line with newfound knowledge, the whole family can flourish. Women who feel guilty about studying can remember these advantages when the HE journey is difficult.

Children's relationships with their father can be enhanced and transformed by their spending more time together. Yet, although the children benefit when they rely on their father as well as their mother, some women struggle with this shift in identity as a parent and may even feel jealous, torn between wanting to study and wanting to mother, wanting childcare support to be able to study and wanting to be with their children. This chapter outlines the ways HE affects relationships with partners and children. Changes to family relationships can include transformations to parenting techniques, enhanced educational opportunities for children, increased friction for some partners and strengthened relationships for others. This is often dependent on whether women students connect or separate their studies and home life. Women who actively connect home and study seem to gain more support from their partners, which can make studying easier.

Strategies to support the changing relationship with your partner and children

The following strategies have been found helpful in supporting changing relationships within the family:

- Before starting your course, plan ahead with your partner about adapting routines, childcare and housework.
- Allow time for your relationship to go through a period of transition as you all get used to the new routines and the shifts in your self-confidence.
- Develop strategies to help your family cope with your studies. You may choose to connect your studies with your family so that it becomes a shared family experience. If you experience conflict you may wish to separate your studies from family life. Or you may choose a mix of separating and connecting depending on what works and when.
- If you feel your studies are creating barriers and resentment between you and your partner and you chose to *separate* your studies from family life to minimize the impact, you should create spaces where you can share your studies with friends or your peer group. Doris found her father-in-law very supportive; this enabled her to practise her new debating skills without alienating her partner.
- Role changes in families can cause additional pressure for your partner, so be aware of the strain of HE studies on both of you. Finding ways together to reduce both of your workloads can create a shared goal.
- Studying often takes away time with your partner, but two strategies were identified that worked. You can either adopt the strategy of a 'date day/night' to create a space in the week to catch up or you can regard the sacrifice of time together as a temporary cost in the shared pursuit of completing your HE studies.
- Be alert to the signs and symptoms of stress in you or your partner and seek support from a healthcare professional if necessary.
- Recognize that feeling guilty is common when trying to be a mum who studies. This is a normal part of studying (see Chapter 7).

- Regard the time the children spend away from you with other family members as beneficial to their other relationships rather than as detrimental to yours.
- Don't be afraid to use your new skills and confidence to positive effect for the family and to support your children educationally.

Chapter 6

Effects on wider relationships

I feel with my parents, I don't know, I can see the pride in me now, I can see it, I think it's probably always been there but I can actually see it now and feel it ... I don't think it changes how I act but it's a nice feeling. You think, so well I am alright then ... you don't feel you have quite so much to prove anymore, because you have proved it ... I've come to realize that maybe my parents think there is something particular about me, but I never saw what they saw in me ... I am different in terms of I feel more self-assured now, I have to admit that I'm not stupid.

(Maggie)

Relationships between women and their partners and children are not the only ones affected when women take on HE. The parents of both partners and the couple's friends might also encounter changes. Some will be positive, but it can be difficult to handle any negative effects while already juggling studies and family life.

'HE affected my relationship with Mum and Dad'

Interactions and relationships with parents changed as the women became more dependent on them for childcare or support with study skills or emotional reassurance. As the women's identity changed, so did their personal relationships.

Some women with younger children relied on their parents to help with childcare so they could attend college or study in peace at home. Their parents helped the women to realize that their studies were valued:

They would help you know, if I needed them to watch the kids for a while, my mum and sister would come and help and that was good ... they [children] had their granny so they weren't on their own.

(Heidi)

A few of the students were surprised by the help they received from their parents with study skills, and also emotional support and encouragement. Maggie welcomed her father's support and was motivated by his approval:

> I felt a bit guilty at times [not seeing her parents as much as prior to HE] but my dad comes to see me ... my dad asks me how I am getting on [with study]. He comes around if I am struggling for a chat, and I say, 'I'm stuck!', because he knows how I work and need to talk it out ... He will come and say, 'Tell me' and I'll say, 'You don't know it Dad', and he'll say, 'Tell me!', and I'll tell him and he'll say, 'Now I'm off home, you get that backside over there and type it up!' So actually my dad has made a difference, yes he has.
>
> (Maggie)

Their parents' approval and acceptance of their studies was important to the women. Feeling guilty over the change to family routines and having less time for the family made the women crave their parents' acceptance of their studying, and they greatly valued practical and emotional support from them.

As their identity transformed, the relationships between most of the women and their parents changed too. Some respected their daughter more:

> My dad asks for my advice for a lot of things now, he tends to come to me of all the children [siblings] and with big decisions ... He obviously wants my opinion and that feels really nice.
>
> (Angelina)

The women's raised status in the eyes of their parents was enhanced because they were completing a degree programme. Parents were proud of their daughter and boasted to their friends:

> They [parents] have seen me grow in my determination and self-worth. They didn't make me do this course, I told them I was doing it and they went, 'Yeah, ok, we will see what comes out.' And now all of a sudden it's, 'Wow', and my dad is telling his friends I'm doing really well and he goes to his club and says his daughter is 'doing a degree and is doing really well, and she's actually getting 2.1 grades!'
>
> (Marie)

But almost half the parents were not supportive of their daughters completing HE and felt uncomfortable with the change in her family role. They thought her ambition was selfish so relationships became strained, and this exacerbated the women's feelings of guilt. The parents criticized their daughters on three main grounds: their *health, neglecting household and mothering duties* and the *pressure on their partner* of the additional household or childcare tasks.

Betty told me that her parents were so concerned about her health and stress levels that they tried to stop her from studying by refusing to look after their grandchildren when Betty was at university. Betty had to defer her studies for a short time while she rearranged her childcare:

> They were doing a little bit of childcare for me ... he [Betty's dad] turned around because he saw I was getting stressed out ... and said that he wasn't going to look after Sophie [daughter] any more ... He said, 'You need to take time off and just be a mum again!' ... It's affected my relationship with my mum and dad ... I was relying on them quite a lot for emotional support, I felt my dad pressurized me into it [leaving the course].

Kim's mother was concerned about Kim neglecting what she felt was important, namely household and mothering duties:

> My mum has always been a stay-at-home mum ... she can't comprehend why on earth I would want a degree when I've got children to look after and a house to keep tidy ... She [mum] doesn't really understand at all why I would want to do it and from that comes absolutely no support in time. It's [HE] such a big part of my life and they [parents] don't understand it at all!
>
> (Kim)

Other parents were concerned about how the pressures of study would affect the family:

> She [mother-in-law] helps me out ... as she takes them [children] to school, this has helped me ... Unlike Jon [partner], who has an understanding of why I am doing this, she doesn't get it and thinks I should be at home, cleaning the house and looking after her son and the children. I have always had a good relationship with her ... but the last year I have struggled with it.
>
> (Jennifer)

Although Jennifer received practical support from her mother-in-law, it was only for the sake of the grandchildren – she did not agree with Jennifer studying. So, although she was prepared to help practically, she couldn't support her wholeheartedly. Jennifer and her mother-in-law had conflicting ideas about how to be a mother and partner. Although such differences are not uncommon between the generations, they can come as a surprise to women who have enjoyed a trouble-free relationship with their parents or partner's parents before they embarked on HE.

When women study they have to revise and even abandon some of their ideas of what it is to be a mother, particularly on a practical level. Kim sees that her priorities have changed and are at now at odds with her mum's, causing conflict and disconnection between them:

> We do have completely different personalities, or maybe similar personalities but different priorities.

Most of the women sought reassurance and pride from their parents about entering HE, so they needed to connect them with their studies (Edwards, 1993a):

> The people that are really delighted are my parents ... so you see, parental respect ... I've craved it all my adult life ... and my dad is really proud of me.
>
> (Marie)

> My mum died when I was 20 ... I don't really see my dad a lot and I just wanted somebody to feel proud of me ... So for Jon [partner] and the kids to see me achieve something for me is good ... my biggest aim is for them to see me graduate, not just the children but Jon's mum as well, because I think that graduation will make her think, 'Well she did do something that was actually quite big.'
>
> (Jennifer)

The women with primary school or pre-school aged children all lived near their own or their partner's parents, which meant that childcare support could be found. However, it was their parents' approval of their studies that mattered most. These findings suggest that women need to feel that their studies are accepted by their loved ones, as this diminishes their feelings of guilt about juggling HE studies and family life and makes the sacrifices easier to bear.

Almost half the women experienced a disconnection with their parents because they couldn't discuss their studies with them and found this barrier between them difficult:

> She [mum] never says to me, 'How are you, how is the studying going?' which is kind of hurtful in a way really ... I would like her to be proud of me.
>
> (Doris)

> She [mum] doesn't really understand at all why I would want to do it and from that comes absolutely no support … My dad is very neutral on the subject, he doesn't really say anything.
>
> (Kim)

Like Doris and Kim, many women want to be able to discuss their educational achievements with their parents and share the journey. Drawing only disinterest or negative responses from their parents can add to the guilt they already feel (see Chapter 7). When parents are negative, finding other sources of support becomes important, such as friendships.

Friendships

As their friends saw the women's identity change, some friendships grew apart, while others grew stronger. Friends as well as family noticed how HE led to changed viewpoints on various topics and greater self-assurance:

> I went over to my friend's house for coffee on Friday and she has got a lot of issues at the moment, she said that I'm really good at listening now, but also at giving the alternative perspective.
>
> (Angelina)

> I've got friends that I only meet once a year or eighteen months and when I last met them they said, 'You've just really blossomed and you kind of know who you are', so that was good. My friends are viewing me as more confident now generally.
>
> (Maggie)

> I think I am different around them [friends], I'm still me but I think that sometimes I have to stop myself and think, 'Hang on Heidi, you don't need to talk in that much depth'. Perhaps, if I'm talking about things then I start going off on a tangent about things I have learnt on my degree … and I think, 'No! What are you going on about?'
>
> (Heidi)

Heidi struggles to suppress her enthusiasm for her studies when she is with her friends; although she is passionate about her new knowledge, she is aware that her friends may not be quite so interested. She developed a strategy of adapting her conversations to suit those around her but found it difficult, because she didn't want to bore or overload them with detail but she had to respond when they asked for her advice. Heidi found that this created blurring between the roles of friendship and professional advice:

> They almost expect you to [offer professional childcare advice], it's hard to explain, because they know how far I've gone in my studies and that I am nearer the latter part now, they almost expect me to be slightly more knowledgeable, more professional and I think sometimes you do feel that you have got to uphold that ... they ask you what sort of things you think or you must know this, what do you think?

Kim found friendships breaking down because of the differences between them since she began studying. Having less in common with her friends now put a strain on their relationship:

> I used to have friends *(laughs)* ... I have less in common with friends I spent time with before. I haven't maintained very many, or had any really, friendships which were a big part of my life really ... as a friend [before HE] I used to have more time to dedicate to friendships and socializing with other people outside of the family but I don't see friends anymore really. I find my old friends a lot less interesting ... my interests have changed ... Sometimes I think I may have jumped up a social bracket.

This is not an unusual situation. Some women feel they have changed so much that their previous interests and conversations are no longer relevant. Like Kim, women may feel a little lonely:

> I suppose I am a little bit lonely ... I think it's definitely made me isolated, I've had to isolate myself ... I don't know if now I have like an internal struggle about that because I feel on the outside of that and I do feel on the outside of where I used to be as well so I feel like a little bit in between ... It is possibly the amount of time that I spend reading and sort of maybe understanding things on a different level that I wouldn't have understood before.

However, Kim, rather like Esme and Doris with their partners, saw this loneliness as only temporary. They were aware that working towards a degree was a journey of self-discovery and they would end up a different person from the one who started out. So they were able to put friendships and relationships on hold.

Jennifer offers us a final perspective on friendships that touches on many of the stories. She found that, although she had less time for her friends and neglected them a little, they were still a strong part of her support network and she relied on them for encouragement. Jennifer felt that her friends also gave her a social life away from her studies and family, where she had time to relax from the pressures of her life and ease her stress:

> The friends thing has also taken a bit of a back seat as I have not had as much free time, umm, so catching up with them has been quite tricky, so at times this has been a bit difficult because that's probably a bit of my 'get out' clause, which I haven't really had much of lately. And that is what tends to keep me sane a little bit as well, and that had a big impact on it as well … They [friends] were more supportive than family members … and they keep saying, 'I don't know how you're doing it, I could not do it', a lot of sort of admiration and stuff, which kept me going.

In sum, HE study may transform a woman's identity and change her relationship with her parents. They might be proud and encouraging, or concerned and disapproving about their daughter's identity transformation and changed approach to motherhood, to the point even of withdrawing their childcare.

Friendships changed too, for better or worse. The best were motivating, and afforded a welcome distraction from pressures of home and study. Although they were important, the women could let them go while they were studying, as maintaining relationships in their families mattered even more.

Strategies to sustain support from family and friends

Women trying to cope with studying and family can be sure they aren't alone in feeling anxious and conflicted. Although everyone's experience is unique, you will relate to many of the stories that emerged in my study. Sharing your experiences with others and having a reflective approach will help you as your partner, family and friends adjust to changes brought about by your studies. The following strategies may help:

- Recognize that your priorities may differ from those of your parents and this may create conflict or negativity.
- Just as your relationship with your partner may need a period of adjustment, so may the relationship with your parents.
- Be aware that not everyone will be as passionate as you are about your new ideals and subjects of interest. Find people who can share your interests and engage in debate and don't force the issue with people who clearly do not share your passions.

- Follow Heidi's strategy of adjusting her discussions to fit the people involved.
- If your parents are unsympathetic, take time out with friends who want to share the journey with you.
- You are likely to make new friends on your course; they may share with you the reactions of their own parents and friends. Having a network of support can alleviate the kind of loneliness Kim experienced when she no longer had much in common with her old friends.

Part Four

Feeling guilty

4

I feel really guilty for putting this extra huge weight on the whole family.

(Kim)

I have learnt as well to manage my time and I know I can do about an hour then I get up and go do something then I come back to it. I've kind of learnt techniques of how I study best.

(Doris)

Guilt is a huge stumbling block for many women on an HE course. My mature women students talk with me and each other about feeling guilty. Spending less time than they would like with their family or on studying makes them feel guilty and frustrated. So strongly does it affect women who study that I've devoted this chapter to it, as the emotional effects of juggling cannot be underestimated. Women often manage to adjust to the practicalities of studying and even learn to cope with less sleep. But what they find hardest to cope with is the feeling of letting the family down, of not being there in the way that they want to be and of putting themselves first.

Chapter 7

Juggling time and feeling guilty

I just felt I wasn't spending as much time with them [children] and I was always busy … I was always trying to push them away because I wanted to sit down and study so yeah, there has been a hell of a lot of guilt in the last 12 months.

(Jennifer)

HE study changes people's identity. It increases their knowledge, self-belief and self-confidence, and can improve their parenting. But women often feel a deep sense of guilt centred on feeling that they are neglecting the family.

Causes of guilt

For most of the women in my research, their guilt was mainly centred on having less time for their children, partner or wider family. The women believed they were neglecting their duties as a mother by using family time for HE study.

Hilary's feelings of guilt were not about children, however, as she always prioritized time with them over her HE studies. Instead, she *felt guilty because she didn't have enough time for her studies*. She had decided that her studies were less important than the needs of her family and chose not to cut back her time with them, but she often wished she could spend more time studying without feeling that she was neglecting them. So, whatever way you look at it, guilt features large in women's accounts of combining HE study with family life.

Before embarking on HE, the women in this research were the main carers for the children and, generally, responsible for attending to the household tasks. Having to divide their time between study, family, household tasks and, in many cases, part-time paid work was very difficult. Kim illustrates this with a metaphor:

In the first year I felt like I'd had a baby, I felt like it was that tiring, that I'd just given birth to another child *(laughs)*. It just impacted the routine in that same sort of way that when you have a newborn baby in your house, it just completely threw everything up in the air and didn't really ever go back to how it was before.

Kim makes the interesting point that life 'didn't really ever get back to how it was before'. This is so true of HE study. As we've seen, women transform their confidence levels, self-image, routines and relationships, and the family dynamics change accordingly. Jennifer felt that family life would change for ever as the family learnt to adapt to being less accessible:

I don't think it would go back to how it was before [HE]. But them [children] being older as well will have an impact on that but I think they will be used to me not being there as much.

Although the women see that their HE studies can offer positive educational benefits for themselves and their children, growing independence skills for the children and positive changes in how they parent, they still worry about the potential negative effects of their compromises and how to juggle duties. The women said that they felt they were putting their own interests above the family, and this added to their feelings of guilt:

I do feel a little bit guilty about it all because I'm doing it for me; it's all for me isn't it?

(Angelina)

They felt responsible for causing stress by disrupting family life because they chose to study:

My house has always been like a pre-school [previously to HE] … I suppose that had an impact, I haven't done as much as I should, or that I am used to doing, because I have not had the time. But that is more of the guilt on my part, for the children and for him [partner].

(Jennifer)

Both Edwards (1993a) and Hughes (2002) view HE as a 'greedy institute of time'. Women who study can relate to this, feeling as though their HE studies are a time monster eating away greedily at the time they need for others, and that they need an extra day in the week just to keep on top of it all.

Managing guilt through managing time pressures

To overcome this problem women learn to manage their daily routine effectively so they do what they consider is essential to be a good mother.

Heidi prioritized what she saw as the essential tasks of care and educational demands, although they ate into the time for playing with her children. Encouraging them to play independently was new to her. Esme saw spending time away from the house with her teenage daughter as essential. Every woman student will make her own choices over what elements of motherhood cannot be abandoned. Things like housework or spending time with friends may not be essential to one's identity or well-being, but being a good mother is:

> When I started my degree, it was an issue for me because my routine and organization did, at times, become out of my control. And I didn't like that, I didn't like the house getting messy and then I thought after a while I just had to let it go and so that was hard for me I think … it was really hard to let it go, but it had to go. That was the first thing I had to drop because I couldn't drop my studies and I couldn't drop the children's health and things like that, could I? … I did what I had to do, like the cooking and things like that, but after that, you know, it was the study and things like that really.
>
> (Heidi)

> I realize how much I can achieve by being organized and juggling things … It is my time really to get a grip on everything in my life and everything I want to be … I want to be a good mum.
>
> (Angelina)

Spending time away from the family can make women feel guilty, as can the sense of being distant from the family while pre-occupied with study. Such feelings affect how women students see themselves as a mother and a partner:

> So there was other guilts because I'm last minute.com when it came to the deadlines, they [children] are really sporty and in football tournaments and this that and the other and I would have to get to the point where I can't come and watch this match and I would feel guilty … it was a juggling act because I was there all the rest of the time I've realized but I did feel guilty but that was my fault, if I'd managed my time better and I wouldn't have had that stress at the end of the module.
>
> (Maggie)

Some are torn between the desires to study and to be with their families or do things for them. Where once the needs of their children were the priority, now studying creates conflict and they feel selfish for seeking to achieve a degree. Maggie felt her own study habits seemed inadequate and robbed her of time she could be spending with her children.

Women are surprised at how much time their studies take: 'Think how long you expect writing your essay to take, then double it, you may be closer to the truth!'

> I don't think he [partner] realized how much it [HE studies] was going to impact on everything and how much time it takes, he does get annoyed, with the time that I spend sometimes.
>
> (Jennifer)

> No, there's no hiding from it [HE studies] and if something happens like there is a school play or something I don't just duck out of work and go back to work I have to then fill that time, I have to find that time to study and then that time for him [partner]. It is then our time that goes so it is harder.
>
> (Kim)

Instead of focusing on their studies, they worry about how their family are coping without them or else worry about neglecting their studies while they're playing with their children:

> I mean there were still sometimes when I stopped studying to play with the children, I thought, 'I really wanted to finish that! [studying]', and then I felt guilty because when I was doing stuff with them [playing with the children] I was still thinking about studying.
>
> (Jennifer)

Women feel guilty about not having enough time for their family, guilty when the family seem to cope without them, guilty about managing their time ineffectively and guilty over putting their own career needs first. And not only is guilt self-inflicted; other people can add to it.

Over half the women in my study were made to feel guilty about studying by their parents, who thought they should be content with the role of mother. But only two women – Doris and Marie – faced conflict with their partners, which goes against much previous research (Edwards, 1993a; Merrill, 1999; Schuller *et al.*, 2004). Even a recent study by Brooks (2015) found there were assumptions by partners that student mothers in the UK would carry the main responsibility for childcare. This is supported by research by the Fatherhood Institute (2016) showing that the responsibility for childcare and housework still rests more heavily on women. Yet, my research found that most of the women felt their partners supported their studies and that even if they felt neglected or under pressure from household tasks or childcare, they did not want their wives to quit the course. Opposition and pressure came from parents, not partners. Clearly it was their parents who defined what it is to be a mother, and conflict arose when their daughters stepped outside the expected role. This surprised the women, who had hoped for practical and especially emotional support from them.

Finding ways to feel less guilty

My research revealed six key strategies the women devised to help them reduce their feelings of guilt. One was to avoid studying in front of their children. Those whose children were young studied while they were at school:

> I had a Wednesday, that was my study day, and I wouldn't let anyone get in the way of that … That was very precious time and I think that's how I managed to juggle all the roles, because that time when my children were in school, so I didn't feel guilty that I was sitting at a table from 9 to 3 solidly studying, there was no guilt involved there because that was allocated to study time. And by doing that I felt I kept a handle on everything, because I didn't feel I neglected the children.
>
> (Angelina)

Some women like to get into the flow of studying and devote a large chunk of time to getting to grips with a topic. Angelina studied like this: not only was it effective but she felt less guilty about neglecting her children. Other women prefer studying in shorter, energetic bursts. But few could choose their study time according to their learning preference but had to fit studying into whatever time their family's needs permitted.

Knowing that their mother went to 'big school' positioned them as educational role models for their children. Seeing their studies from this angle helped the women feel less guilty, as studying was therefore for the good of the children. Taking this position makes it a 'rational choice' (Scott, 2014: 625) for the women to develop their knowledge and skills, as it will enhance their well-being but also that of their children.

As a woman student, you are a mother whose accumulation of cultural capital and attitude towards education benefit your children's educational aspirations (Davies *et al.*, 2014). This position enables you to see your studies as a choice that helps your children rather than being a selfish decision. You may feel less guilty and you also have a stronger argument against those who don't value or accept your studying. When the women saw themselves as educational role models, failure was not an option! This proves to be highly motivating when you are struggling with coursework or worried about how you spend your time:

> There have been times when I have struggled and thought, 'I can't do this', but there have never been times when I have thought of not doing it ... I wouldn't want my children to see me pulling out of it.
>
> (Jennifer)

> I think, them seeing me do this and being a mum has carried me on, you cannot quit a course when you are a mum ... you cannot walk away from it ... you are an example to them.
>
> (Maggie)

Ensuring that the children were spending time with other family members, such as their father or grandparents, also lessened some of the guilt. The women could see that the children enjoyed spending time with other family members, and how family relationships were strengthened.

Strategies of studying when the children were not around and of having them spend time with other family members were effective as they allowed the women to conceal some of their study time from their children so there was less cause for resentment.

During school holidays, when they needed to study intensively while the children were at home, the women made focused additional quality time for their children by designating clear study times and 'activity/play' times. Some of them had the children measuring study time with a stop watch so they knew their quality activity/play time with mum was ring-fenced:

> The main times I study in front of them are in holiday times because study doesn't stop because they're off school. My compromise is that I say, 'I need to get an hour or so done here, if you can play really nicely and then mummy will take you out afterwards' ... they don't complain about it they know I'm doing it for a reason, because I want to be a teacher one day.
>
> (Angelina)

I do try and do things with them [children] when I have to study in the holidays or on Saturdays, I put it on my eldest daughter and say, 'Look, when it's eleven o'clock tell me to stop!', and she would just clock watch literally, 'Ten minutes Mum', 'Eight minutes … Stop!', I'd stop, I'd get up and get them to choose what they wanted to do … they seemed to like telling me [when the study time was over] … I mean there were still sometimes when I stopped I was thinking just like I really wanted to finish that and then I felt guilty because when I was doing stuff with them I was still thinking about it.

(Jennifer)

The women felt responsible for balancing the needs of the family with their need to study so that neither was neglected. Their perceptions of what it was to be 'a mother' guided them in their decisions. They wanted to show they could manage HE and family life and succeed in both:

If there was a problem you know and an issue and stress in the family I'd probably think it was my fault for not giving everyone enough time or putting too much pressure on my husband to do things when I should be doing it … If I can balance it all and keep everybody happy and that's kind of what I hold to myself, is that you know I need to do this for myself and why shouldn't I?

(Angelina)

However much I love my children I have to think about my future as well … I want to be able to help my own children financially and academically and that is what drives me more than anything.

(Heidi)

Women use various strategies of separating or connecting their studies (see Chapter 5). At the end of her programme, Maggie reflects on how she struggled to manage her time and her feelings and how she overcame them:

My early experience as an HE student was one of being in an almost permanent state of playing 'catch up'; I was either striving to meet academic deadlines, work demands, or trying to be the perfect mother and wife. Over time, I learned that I could relinquish some of the guilt associated with being unable to be all things to everyone whilst studying, and in doing so, began to enjoy the process of exploring just how clever I was capable of being. I learned that it was ok to say, 'No', and almost acceptable to put my own needs first, although I never quite managed to do so without an element of guilt! HE studies taught me to value myself as an individual and learning to do so led to my realizing how valuable others considered me.

(Maggie)

This chapter examined women's guilty feelings about having too little time for children, partner or household tasks when studying. To overcome these feelings, the women adopted practical strategies, allocating their time differently, avoiding studying in front of their children, ensuring that others were caring for them. And they justified their study to the family – and themselves – by pointing out the benefits: educational role modelling, raising their children's aspirations and the prospect of financial gain through an enhanced future career. Being a mother was still of prime importance but motherhood is reconsidered, transformed and reconstructed through HE. Guilt should not stand in the way of studying: HE study develops women's self-confidence and they value this. But there need to be practical strategies in place for managing time and living with guilt.

Strategies for managing time and dealing with guilt

I have gathered these strategies and co-constructed them in collaboration with women students over the years. I can identify only a few of the original sources as most emanated from discussions in class. Here I draw them together in an accessible form for students.

Strategies for dealing with guilt

- Recognize the benefits of studying for the whole family – such as improving higher educational aspirations through role modelling, supporting your children's education from a position of greater knowledge, a likely hike in income with a career change, and the positive changes in family dynamics and relationships.
- Share your journey with the family – many of the women in this study talk about how their children are proud of their achievements, for example Marie:

> When you are feeling guilty try and remember that you will be a source of inspiration and are setting a positive example to your children about what it is possible to achieve.

- Allocate regular quality time with each family member. Some women students trade an hour's uninterrupted study time for play and a picnic in the park or go off shopping with a teenager in order to reconnect.

- Conceal your study time and the pressures of study from children – some women adopt the strategy of only studying when their children aren't around – but then partners may feel neglected!
- Recognize that you cannot do it all – when you add studying at HE level to what is already a busy schedule something has to give. You need to decide what this is. Is there a committee you are on, a club you attend or obligations that can be put on hold while you are studying? Can you delegate any tasks at work or at home to ease the load? Students talked about how the house is not as clean or the Christmas cake no longer homemade, or stepping down from sports coaching for a while – things they are willing to let slide rather than seeing family relationships suffer.

Strategies to support time management and secure study time

- Make clearly defined study times when you know you won't be interrupted. This might be for one whole day a week when the children are at school, or two evenings a week when they are in bed or someone takes over the bedtime routine.
- Ring-fence and protect these study times – get your family on board with making 'Do not disturb' signs and protecting your 'quiet time'. Switch off all social networks and distractions, ignore the housework, and focus on study. If you do lose this designated time, plan another time in the week. This discipline helps you keep on top of your work.
- It takes planning to create study time in the school holidays. Get the children to allocate time with a stop watch and have clearly defined study times and family times. The trick is to stop when agreed; this will build up trust and help alleviate the guilt!
- Discover your study weakness and work with it, for example Maggie says:

> I am a procrastinator ... always. So I learned to accept that and made sure when a deadline was looming that I budgeted in time to allow me to clear the ironing, have a long day out, clean the bathroom, and generally avoid any kind of study; I literally spent time deliberately eradicating every possible distraction so that for at least the last fortnight leading up to a deadline there really was nothing to do but the assignment.

- Secure additional study times when assignments are due in – ask for support from other family members to help with childcare at home or to take the children out for the day.
- Don't leave everything to the last minute – it is vital to keep up with your assignments and tasks because being a mum means having to deal with unexpected family emergencies, as Esme notes:

> Don't leave anything until the final hours, whether it's coursework or revision; you are more likely than the younger students to have a last-minute drain on your time, I should know I learnt some hard lessons.

- Don't worry about the next assignment – one step at a time is a useful strategy, as Maggie says:

> Each assignment brings new challenges and avenues of exploration. Focus only on the assignment in hand; the next one will come soon enough! I would have found it too daunting to look at the bigger picture and investigate every assignment I was expected to do throughout each academic year. I coped better by focusing on one at a time.

- Set clear and realistic targets for what you want to achieve in each study time – colour code these as green for go (essential), yellow (desirable) and red (stop – do not attempt till other tasks are completed). This will help you to stay focused and achieve each task a step at a time. But if you can't get started on the task you planned, do something else rather than waste the time.
- Select appropriate tasks for the situation – consider carefully how much time you have and plan accordingly. Tasks such as proofreading can be picked up and put down (e.g. when waiting to collect a child from sport); searching for online journals can be saved for when you want to be around the family but can be multi-tasking.
- Always have a notebook, post-its, a pen and a study book with you – these can be used for those lightbulb moments or snatched time while waiting for something or someone. I know one student who had a 'lightbulb moment' at night but rather than wake her partner with the light, she grabbed a pen and noted her thoughts on her arm in the dark! Although this is not a recommended strategy, writing things down when you think of them is advisable. Or you can record your thoughts on a mobile phone or dictaphone as Maggie did:

In my experience, your clearest thoughts and academic arguments will emerge in the middle of the night in place of a decent sleep. Getting a dictaphone was amazing, I didn't have to keep my eyes open while recording my thoughts, and when I woke up the next day, I had some great areas of thought to explore further.

- Keep effective notes – although this might initially feel time consuming, keeping records of links to references and accurate notes is essential for essays. Some students find that emailing links to notes or references and emailing regular copies of their work to their inbox prevents losing work.
- Create a study area – having a designated space for study also helps with time management. A desk is ideal, away from distractions, but many women manage to study on the kitchen table. Have a box or tray to store your books and resources so you can remove them quickly and keep them safe. If you can, make full use of your day at the university by organizing to stay late and work in the library.
- Trust in your ability – don't be afraid to start a piece of work; avoid procrastinating. Don't be afraid to begin something out of sequence; getting started can be the hardest part.

Part Five

Gaining support through
family capital

I think my biggest strength is my family ... that has always been solid, but it has impacted when you are really stressed and everyone has adapted around me, but I only think that's because I have that strong network naturally around me.

(Christina)

I am feeling a little snowed under with it all at the moment, especially with Fiona [daughter] being so unwell. David [partner] is very busy and offering very little in the line of help and support. So I feel very put upon and cross that he gets annoyed when I say I am tired and need to go to bed early. I cannot do it all – work, study, mother, housekeeper, gardener, cook fresh meals etc. I feel very old and dry. I need some TLC and rest!

(Doris)

During your higher education programme, support is essential. The families of most women students help with childcare, household tasks and offer emotional support and encouragement. Having a network of support of the kind identified by Christina greatly helps with juggling studies and family life.

Appropriate support can determine whether or not a woman succeeds on her programme or constantly struggles. The types of support on offer within families can usefully be described as family capital.

Chapter 8

Gaining family capital: 'I could not have done it without my family'

He [partner] is so supportive of me, I think if I couldn't go home and have him as a sounding board then I don't think I would have got through it. And also, with the juggling of the roles the fact that he is taking on more this year has made a massive difference, yes, definitely ... I see it as my husband, you know, as the one that got me through this.

(Angelina)

This chapter develops the concept of family capital to show the role of the family in supporting women through their HE studies. It illustrates my model of family capital and the support it provides. The stories of the women reveal the benefits of family capital as well as the difficulties experienced when it is lacking.

Bourdieu's concept of capital embraced the cultural, social, economic and symbolic (Bourdieu, 1986 and 1991). Capital is the 'goods and resources' that can benefit an individual or the asset to be cashed in (Jenkins, 2002: 85). It would include sharing study skills, access to finances for study, and social networks that aid educational progress. Bourdieu (1991) emphasized that if access to capital is limited, the outcome is educational inequalities. Women are disadvantaged when they receive no educational, practical or emotional support from their partner or other family.

The concept of family capital includes all forms of capital that 'capture all aspects of investment made by the family' for the benefit of a member (Gofen, 2009: 107), in this case the women students (see Figure 8.1). Within my research, I developed the concept of family capital to include both practical and emotional support strategies. When a woman's family is actively supportive it shows the student that her choice to study is valued, so she doesn't feel so guilty and can explore new possibilities for identity and positional change in the family. In Figure 8.1, I define family capital as four areas of capital support with the thread of time linking them together.

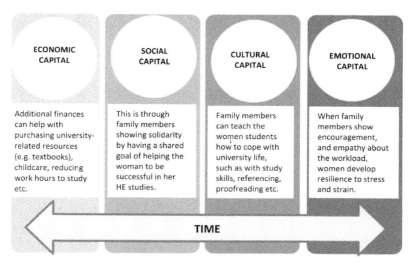

Figure 8.1: My model of family capital for HE women students

These aspects of family capital support a woman in her studies financially, practically and emotionally.

My research showed that a woman's HE experiences and consequent transformation cannot easily be separated from family life. A change in one part of her life affects the other parts, relationships and routines. We have seen that receiving support from partners, in the form of housework or childcare, can enhance her capacity to study, and transform children's relationships with their fathers.

Relationships between the women and their parents change too, whether evoking her parents' pride and emotional support or their disapproval and withdrawal. When emotional or practical support from a partner or parents is lacking, the student constantly has to negotiate time to study and may also feel greater guilt and emotional turbulence, although some women who lack support become more determined to prove they are capable of achieving this goal on their own, as Doris, Hilary and Marie did.

The concept of family capital is useful in showing how to achieve the end goal of the woman succeeding in her HE studies. Family capital will be used to consider 'the aspects of investment made by the family' (Gofen, 2009: 107) for the benefit of the woman student and her family as a whole. To express this in financial terms, the contribution of time or skills they give is so as to acquire future benefits such as a better career pathway for the student, her personal growth or her improved earning capacity.

Different aspects of capital provided by the family

My study adds emotional capital to Bourdieu's (1986) original categories of capital; it is more appropriate to women than his 'symbolic capital', which is about honour, status and prestige. And 'time' is a strong thread that links all forms of family capital, as women students have to rely on the time given by others to allow them to study.

Cultural capital

Cultural capital is shared when family members know about the HE system and can help women fit into university life (Winkle-Wagner, 2010). The women valued the cultural capital that their partners gave, such as proofreading their work or helping to develop study or IT skills. The women saw this practical help as an endorsement of their study for a degree:

> One of the things he [partner] said was, 'I notice that I don't have to check your spelling as much as I used to when you started', and he's noticed my writing is a lot better and flows more easily when he does read it now so I think he's quite impressed, you know ... I think he was as supportive as he could be. Especially I think correcting my grammar and things like that ... he was supportive like that.
>
> (Esme)

Those whose partners had themselves studied at university benefited from stories about their own experiences and their understanding of how intense and time-consuming HE study is. In other cases, the women turn to their friends who share in how they are feeling and value what they are doing. Some find support from their children who are or had been at university. These children brought capital through supporting the development of study skills, discussing their mother's assignments and valuing what their mothers have achieved. Such recognition is a huge boost to emotional capital:

> She [Maggie] didn't know what things meant, uni [university] terms and things like this, I remember them [wife and son] chatting and she just couldn't grasp what these words were and what to do and over time he taught her basically about the world of the university if you like!
>
> (Ross)

> Rob [son] has helped because Rob has been doing a degree and
> we have shared it ... he has made me value what I'm doing by the
> fact that he has valued what I have done.
>
> (Maggie)

Esme was able to identify better with her teenage daughter because she was
studying at college. Studying at the same time strengthened their relationship
and gave them both a better understanding of the difficulties study presents:

> I suppose it's because I'll come back from university ... and I'll
> know, because she's doing A Levels, so I'll know terminology that
> they use for A Levels and things like that and computers, I'm
> much more computer literate you know ... I think she sees me
> more as sort of an equal now, because we are both studying and
> I'll say, 'Oh this is really hard', and she'll say, 'Think of me I have
> got about four assignments you know, think of me, I'm struggling
> too!' So we've got that little bit in common, you know we are
> learning together. I think she finishes her A Levels when I finish
> this as well so it's quite nice to be supportive and that she can
> come to me, so yeah, I think our relationship has been brought
> closer, not that we weren't close before ... And I think I have
> empathy as well with how hard it is studying.

Very few of the women spoke about receiving cultural capital from their
parents. Maggie benefited from study support from her father, which
surprised her as her father had no experience of HE. But he was able to
develop her study skills by giving his daughter the time and opportunity to
talk through her studies. Even more important was having her assignment
difficulties listened to and recognized. This cultural capital can be provided
by those without HE experience. Her father's encouragement gave Maggie
the emotional support she needed to keep going.

Economic capital

Some women benefit from economic capital in the form of money, pooling
their resources with partners so they can cut back on their employment
hours. Some families in this research endured a reduction in income; in
other cases, it was the man who worked shorter hours so he could assist
with childcare or household tasks:

> Well, I have asked to do the hours [reduced hours], I am able to
> do this in my work. So they have let me have these hours so that

> I can be home at this time so if I couldn't do that then maybe she couldn't have gone to Uni ... but with the Uni work as well it's worked out brilliantly, if I was doing shifts we'd be in trouble.
>
> (Alan)

Economic capital enabled students to buy more resources such as textbooks. Access to study materials (Webb *et al.*, 2002) was more important than buying in childcare as many of the children were already at pre-school or school. Being able to study from home allows the women to balance family life and study more easily so having resources to hand was invaluable. Often the women snatch nuggets of time when they can, picking up the study materials and dropping them at a minute's notice:

> It's taken over the family life, the home, because there are books everywhere, once it's set out on the table it stays there until I've finished.
>
> (Jennifer)

Social capital

Bourdieu (1991) saw social capital as having access to a network of relationships that aided success with education. The women did not discuss social networks (Bourdieu, 1991), but they did discuss the bonding and solidarity aspect of social capital, as described by Putnam (2000) and Coleman (1998). Some partners had experience of HE so understood the demands of study. These couples developed their solidarity over the shared goal. The women who didn't feel their partners believed in what they were doing concealed or tried to justify their studies. The women are more likely to benefit from economic or cultural capital than social capital as it is easier to provide money or practical study skills. What was most evident was the emotional capital on offer within families that the women drew upon.

Emotional capital

Emotional capital is made up of the 'emotional resources – such as support, patience and commitment – built over time particularly within families' (Zembylas, 2007: 451). Emotional responses such as resilience, motivation and high self-esteem are developed in families from childhood; it is these attributes that develop a woman's emotional capital. Emotional capital is often seen mainly as being provided by women and consumed by men and children (Burke and Jackson, 2007); women give emotional support, men and children take it.

My findings show otherwise. Emotional capital offered by the partners, who showed the women sensitivity and understanding, helped to develop the students' emotional capital so they could build motivation and resilience to the stress of HE study. The women appreciated their partners acknowledging the pressure they were under and not asking them to give up:

> He [partner] never in any way asked me to stop, what he did do was say, 'Are you sure you are alright? You know it's not the be all and the end all', and I said, 'Yes', but it was just that not knowing in that first two assignments that whatever I submitted would actually pass, does that make sense? And I really thought, I used to think, 'Oh my goodness, it's not going to pass, I am not at the right academic level', in those first few assignments and he was saying, 'Yes, you can, you can do it'.
>
> (Christina)

Having their studies respected and supported in this way reaffirms the women's inherent self-belief and gives them incentive to continue. They thrive when their partners show concern, express pride and encourage them to succeed. Although some of the relationships were put under stress because of the HE course (Angelina and Bradley; Esme and Alan; Kim and Matt), the couples drew on the reserves of emotional capital already developed during their mutually supportive relationships (Feenay and Lemay, 2012). The women believed that this enabled their partners to respond to their own changing feelings and emotions; for example, sharing her joy when she passed an assignment, or encouraging her to persevere if she doubted her own ability:

> She has what she calls her stressful moments when she has got to get stuff [assignments] in and sometimes I bring her back down to earth and say, 'You know you are probably sixty per cent ahead of everyone else, just relax', and also sometimes I'll kick her ass and say, 'You're not going to be watching TV tonight, you've got to work', ... she has her moments when she starts doubting herself, you know I give her a bit of a reality check and say how great she is and look at the marks you know.
>
> (Bradley)

Emotional support enhanced the women's emotional capital when their partners endorsed and defended their study to their parents and in-laws:

> I have said to Jon [partner] quite a few times now, I've never said things to Jon about his mother before and I said, 'If your mother says that [disapproving of HE studies] one more time, I'm gunna …' And I think he has noticed her saying things … and at times he has stuck up for me. And normally he would let it go … She thinks I should be more organized and Jon says, 'She possibly can't get any more organized! Else she wouldn't be able to do it!'
>
> (Jennifer)

Through such camaraderie and encouragement, the women were able to bear the intensity of balancing their study, home life and work life.

The woman's children were also part of her emotional capital. Women who had viewed their role of mother as responding to and meeting their children's needs (Lawler, 2000) were surprised to find they permitted themselves to have needs they wanted their children to meet. When their children enquired about their studying, the women's emotional capital was enriched by telling them about it. When they took pride in their mother's achievements, the women felt justified in spending so much time away from them. Although they still felt guilty, their emotional capital helped them justify it to themselves:

> I think they [children] respect me for that [studying] … and they ask me about it and they don't mind me studying, asking if I'm studying today. 'You doing your study Mummy on the computer?', and they accept it.
>
> (Angelina)

> There have been times where I could have spent more time with them [children], but they have actually been very understanding about that … they have both said that they are very proud of me.
>
> (Doris)

Not all women can build up emotional capital by receiving emotional support from their partner. However, some can draw on their reserves from childhood and other relationships so as to withstand their partner's lack of emotional support or pride. Having their children share in their success is especially poignant. Marie spoke about how her 6-year-old son asked her how she was doing and celebrated her successful high grades. His interest reassured her that what she was doing was respected and valued by her children and not harmful to them.

In fact I know she's [daughter] enormously proud of me and Oscar [son] loves it [Marie studying] … They tell me they are proud, so when I get the results, Oscar is like, I think he doesn't really know what it means [when he asks what grade she has achieved], but the feeling of success, and the success because I'm happy and I say, 'Yes! I have done it.' Oscar says, 'Yes!'

(Marie)

Time as an aspect of capital

Inevitably, women students with children are time poor. The students in my study spoke about 'wanting more time to study' and 'wanting to spend more time with the family', 'freeing up time', 'time pressures', 'finding time' and being 'time poor'. Bourdieu (1986) views time as a commodity to increase profits. Time investments by family members to take on childcare or household tasks allow women more time to study and achieve. But time is still deemed 'precious' or in 'short supply'. The women felt they were time poor because of being a mother and that HE was a 'greedy institute' that demanded their time (Edwards, 1993a; Hughes 2002). They talked about 'managing time', 'wasting time', 'using time wisely', 'not having as much time', 'having no support in terms of time', 'finding time to study', 'making time' and of study 'taking time away from the family'. Time is seen as precious, something that can be given, taken and obviously used up.

Time is hugely valuable. It underpins and threads through each form of capital. An investment in time made by others is an unwritten endorsement and acceptance of the women's studies. When partners give up their time, be it social time or relaxation time, women see it as approval of their studying.

Some partners who have cultural capital through knowledge of HE study skills assist practically with proofreading and study support. Those who have a cultural awareness of the intensity of HE study encourage the women to be committed to their studies.

The women valued the time their parents and especially their partners gave to childcare and household tasks so they could devote more time to study. The children, too, freed up time for them, playing independently while they studied, and helping with household tasks.

Through having time to study, absorb the subject material and reflect, students are able to develop the transformations that started in lectures. Time gives women a transformational study space to assimilate HE knowledge and reflect on their changing perspectives.

> You do transform your whole depth of thinking, and the evaluation, and all the reflection ... I know that because I have read this, I have read that and you have solid knowledge.
>
> (Maggie)

The women transformed academically within their identity as an HE student but also as a mother and partner within the home because of the change in their roles as a result of the time the partners freed up for them:

> I went from full-time mum to part-time mum because I literally did do all the childhood stuff, you know, literally he [partner] just went to work and came home again and had the playtime and we do share the role a lot more now ... now I feel more equal with him.
>
> (Angelina)

So if women require more time to fit in their studies and there is an expectation or hope that partners will give up some of their time to offer support, how does this work in practice? It is important at this point to consider the effects of giving up time from the perspectives of the partners: what are the costs of producing this aspect of capital for the women to consume? How do partners see giving their time to release family capital? Access to family capital affords women students additional time and permission to study. But providing this is not always easy or welcomed by partners as it can affect their lives, too, in ways they resent:

> But I would have definitely said to the husband and wife think about what you need to do and go through what the changes will be ... So basically if the man wants to change totally his life then they would have to have a period where he would try and learn to cook if he's not doing that yet ... being prepared after work to go straight to the kitchen ... I didn't realize it would go like this ... I don't think we really realized what the work entailed.
>
> (Ross)

Like the other men in this study, Ross found taking on additional household tasks put him under pressure and caused him stress. Nevertheless, the women continued to study:

> All of the changes that have happened in my life and my relationship breaking up and then getting back together and I

actually sort of held onto this [HE study] and I thought to myself, well it must mean a lot for me to really hold on.

(Esme)

Some kept going because of all the investment their partner had made in their study:

There have been so many times I have thought I just can't do it anymore ... he's [partner] the thing that pushes me to keep going because he'll probably never forgive me if I quit ... We have all invested so much into it.

(Kim)

The women regarded their family's investment in their HE studies, the positive educational outcomes for their children (see Chapter 5), their enhanced self-confidence and knowledge as enough to keep them motivated. Although giving up their own time to support the woman was not without its costs, the men may have been willing to 'trade off' (Reay, 2004: 68) their depleted time against future economic gain. One strategy women students use to enlist their partners' support is the prospect of their qualification improving their future career and earnings.

Talking to their partners and listening to the stories of the women revealed three main reasons why men gave their wives cultural, economic, social and emotional capital:

- They had a shared financial goal.
- Both valued education.
- They had a strong relationship.

Having a **shared financial goal** was raised by all the men interviewed and supported by 60 per cent of the women:

It's an investment for the future ... so if it gets her onto the next rung of her career ladder, which hopefully it will, then it's well worthwhile.

(Alan)

So we are both very supportive of each other's dreams ... I see it as a family dream really ... we both agreed that actually there are things that we can do to make that happen.

(Bradley)

Women and their partners may have different reasons for degree-level study. The men believed that studying at HE for personal gain and fulfilment was not reason enough to disrupt family life. Women often undertake HE for reasons of self-confidence and career opportunities (see Chapter 1). Self-fulfilment is sufficient reason but some partners wouldn't agree, as Jennifer's story illustrates:

> I have said that I want it to do it [HE study], to better the job I am in, to be able to move up, to earn more money that is more of what he [partner] understands, and I wanted to get my brain working again, umm, I think that's the bit he struggles with, it is me wanting to do it and he thinks why, because he doesn't do reading or writing he is not that kind of person. That's the bit he didn't kind of get, 'Why would you want to sit with your head in a book, to me that's kind of torture?', he says!

> I have asked him [partner], 'What do you think about me doing it and everything?', and he was like 'Well!' and I thought 'Ok, do I want to know this or not?' *(laughs)*. I said, 'Do you know why I am doing it? Are you happy with me doing it?' And he sort of said, 'Yes', but I wanted him to say, 'I am happy that you are doing it because you want to do it and it's good for you.' But in his sort of way he said, 'I am happy for you to do it but I want to see that it goes somewhere.' I see what he means, basically he means that, 'You are putting this much time and effort into it, I want to know that you are going to earn more money at the end', that kind of thing, whereas I wanted him to say, 'I want you to do it because you want to do it and it's good for you', but that's not quite what I got ... it would have been nice if he'd said, 'You are doing it for you.' So I wasn't really surprised but I was sort of hoping for something different.

Jennifer accepted that her partner had different motives for her studying but that it was enough that he supported her. When a partner realized the impact of the degree on the woman's career prospects, his time and support for her generally followed:

> It was a bit difficult because I would say, 'I've got work to do' ... and it was a tussle. But I think that he [partner] sees the bigger picture and sees where we are aiming for, and what the future is going to be.
>
> (Angelina)

> I see it as a family dream really because again when she [Angelina] came up with the idea of being a teacher she didn't just make the decision without me, she then spoke with me and we both agreed that actually there are things that we can do to make that happen.
>
> (Bradley)

Most partners also **valued education** themselves:

> I have done studying myself so I understand it takes time and again I am very supportive of her doing it.
>
> (Bradley)

> Higher education in his family is quite important, nearly everybody in his family has got a degree ... Matt [partner] thinks, it's for the long term, and it's quite important to him ... so he sees it as being quite a vital part or just an important thing for me to do in life.
>
> (Kim)

Their own cultural capital and value of education affected the social capital on offer (Coleman, 1998). Those who had experienced HE themselves understood and appreciated the time and effort involved better:

> He [partner] has empathy because obviously having studied himself he knows how demanding it can be.
>
> (Esme)

Although a partner who knows very little about higher-level study can generate capital support (see Chapter 7), lack of cultural capital erected a barrier between Doris and her partner, who was unable to deal with her HE study and felt jealous and resentful. Doris felt compelled to hide her studies from her partner (see also Edwards, 1993a) in order to minimize the conflict:

> I do also think there is a little element as well of jealousy there as he hasn't done it, and David [partner] has pretty much done everything, this is something he hasn't done. So he is not able to, I think he almost feels that he can't join in, he can't sit down and he can't share with me even though I want to share with him as he hasn't done it. I don't know if he feels jealous as he hasn't done it, therefore my wife will be more academic than me, I don't think it's that, it's just that he can't share it with me ... So you find ways of doing it without causing too many ripples.

However, the **strength of the relationship** was the key factor underpinning support (this was also true of parents):

> It depends very much like we said before, on the way your relationship works and if the husband or partner is willing to sort of be a bit flexible and change ... You need a strong foundation.
>
> (Bradley)

> You have to have a solid foundation to start with ... we know each other so well, he knew when I was flagging ... I think that is my biggest strength and as far as family is concerned that has always been solid, but it has impacted when you are really stressed and everyone has adapted around me, but I only think that's because I have that strong network naturally around me.
>
> (Christina)

When the couple have a strong and supportive relationship, they deal with the strains involved in studying and the impact on the family together.

Although both the parents and children were able to give some support, it was the partners who were most likely to give most, particularly financial support, through anticipating the financial gain from higher-level qualifications or having a shared career goal, especially when they had a degree themselves. Also, the men in a strong marital relationship were more likely to alleviate the workload when they saw their partner struggle to manage her study, childcare and household tasks.

Parents – 'I would like her [Mum] to be proud of me'

Women also appreciate emotional support from their parents. Chapter 6 showed that, although some women received emotional and practical support and felt that their parents were proud of them, more than half felt that their relationship with their parents had changed for the worse because of their studies. Being a mature student did not fit with their parents' ideal of what it was to be a mother.

In terms of positioning (Harré and van Lagenhove, 1999), women are often fixed in roles that hark back to the past. Many of the women in this study had been the main carers for the children before embarking on the course and the family were used to this. It was accepted as the norm. Becoming a student alongside their role as a parent created conflict with their or their partner's parents. Some of the women's parents tried to influence them to accept that being a mother meant 'being at home' and 'responsible for the children'. They were not interested in their daughter's studies and offered little support. The women were upset by this opposition and lack of encouragement but nonetheless resisted the stereotype of a mother who was available at all times, and continued with their studies.

Such views of an ideal mother could be about the parents' own emotions, personal history and experiences of mothering (Davies and Harré, 1999), which upheld the structuralist gendered roles of women (Parsons, 1959; Young and Willmott, 1973). Although more families have broader views today (Williams, 2004; Morgan, 2011), these shifts might be more of a problem for the older generation than the partners. For the parents' generation, in the 1970s and early 1980s, housework and motherhood often restricted women's career aspirations (Oakley, 2005). Chapter 7 explored the guilt the women felt about spending less time with their family and instead 'putting themselves first'. It appeared that pressures outside the immediate family might have made them feel guilty about their changing identity and role of mother, particularly when their parents were not understanding about their wish to study. Their justification was that studying at university made them a better role model for their children.

The parents, particularly mothers, who considered being an effective mother and homemaker more important than being a mature student were unwilling to help with childcare or to encourage their daughters by sharing their career aspirations. The women tried to deal with this disapproval by explaining why their studies were important to them, or they learned to 'bite my tongue' and accept whatever help parents gave them, or they refused any support from their parents so as to show they could cope without them. Jennifer and her partner tried hard to justify her studies by showing how the family benefited, and ignored the partner's parents' criticism:

> … and the mother-in-law relationship which is slightly strained because of her not understanding why I am doing it and the lack of support because she feels as if I should be at home, so yeah, I'm not quite as tolerant as I was.
>
> (Jennifer)

Jennifer was reassured by her partner's support, as he took on the battle with his mother over her studying:

> I think, my biggest aim is for them to see me graduate, not just the children but Jon's mum as well, because I think that graduation will make her think, 'Well she did do something that was actually quite big.'
>
> (Jennifer)

Betty was determined to complete her studies, even without any support from her parents. Chapter 6 also shows how some family members, for different reasons, struggle with a mother's choice to study:

> It was with the effect on the family [that caused her to leave her studies originally], the person that finally made my mind up to leave was my dad ... Because I've only got my mum and dad here you see and they run a pub and they were doing a little bit of childcare for me ... that left me with the dilemma that not only was she not settling at nursery, but I couldn't and didn't have anyone else to rely on, so he thought that he was doing it for my own good [when her dad refused to help with childcare]. But he was the one that turned around and said, 'No we are not going to do it [childcare] anymore because it's not helping you. You are not, you know, it's making you worse again [mental health illness]. You need to take time off and just be a mum again.' So I'm back to square one! I was struggling with the guilt thing but once he did that, that was the final straw ... Now [returning to HE study] I've got everything sorted out myself and I'm not going to go down there telling them that it's hard and I'm not going to give anything away, I'm just going to get on and do it, so it's affected my relationship with my mum and dad I think. Probably because with the depression and that I was relying on them quite a lot you know for emotional support I suppose but I don't need that anymore, I don't need my dad telling me what I can and can't do.
>
> (Betty)

The impact of family capital on women's educational success

Families with large resources of family capital are in a strong position to accommodate and adjust to the mother's study at HE level. Through having a flexible approach, childcare roles in the family can be switched to accommodate her going to college and provide study times at home and elsewhere.

The men who gave generous family capital encouraged and enabled the woman's HE success. They also offered practical strategies of support:

> He [partner] is so supportive of me ... if I couldn't go home and have him as a sounding board then I don't think I would have got

through it … Also, with the juggling of roles the fact that he is taking on more this year has made a massive difference.

(Angelina)

The things that he [partner] does with the children [childcare and emotional support] are usually when it comes down to me meeting a deadline or not meeting a deadline, he's usually the one that makes it possible.

(Kim)

I think she could have done it but I think she would have found it more difficult without that support.

(Bradley)

Children and parents can also offer encouragement and motivation. This helps alleviate the guilt many women feel when they spend less time with the family to focus on something for themselves (Merrill, 1999; Edwards, 1993a):

If anyone at home was sort of against it, even the kids, it would be hard work for her.

(Ross)

I think I was relying on that quite a lot as well, just that reassurance that he [partner] does want me to do it and that it is ok for me to take myself off and not sit with him in the evenings … You need that kind of, like you say permission and encouragement.

(Kim)

My research found that, with the exception of Doris's family, male attitudes towards housework and childcare had shifted markedly since Edwards' study (1993a). Most were accommodating and supportive. Eighty per cent of the men helped with childcare or household tasks and the women reported that tasks were distributed more fairly. Ross, for example, took on responsibility for household tasks, freeing up Maggie's time. This is contrary to research by Doucet (2006), McFall (2012), the EHRC (2009) and the Fatherhood Institute (2016), but Morgan (2011) found a variety of ways in which the family enacted various roles, and that these constantly changed over time. The women mainly saw their partners as a valuable source of family capital. Although they varied in their capacity to offer cultural capital, all partners could offer emotional support or social capital, encouragement and time.

Hilary's story demonstrates how one student coped without receiving any family capital. Although it is only one story, some of her strategies may be helpful. Hilary is a single parent with 5-year-old twins. Being a mother was the most important part of her identity and she put this above being a student (see Chapter 2). Hilary did not access any family capital. Although she could have gained some social and emotional capital from her brother through conversations on the phone, she forfeited this and used her time with her children and studied once they went to bed. Economic capital could have been beneficial to Hilary in terms of buying childcare support. Yet once she balanced out the cost implications and the time for transport, she realized that she would do as well to study from home with the children around her. She believed that 'it does work as long as I am happy to under-achieve'. Feelings of guilt drove her to work very long days in order to spend the usual time with the children and then study late into the night. She did not want to compromise on her time with them or be so tired that she couldn't be attentive to their needs. But she found one form of support that over time she began to access and rely on:

> I have support and motivation from within and from you [tutor], as part of your educational role. Through showing understanding about the demands of the course and having to juggle it all, and an understanding and awareness of all of the struggles and the demands of the course and the children. You empathize with having children and have understanding as an umbrella. I actually feel that you have given me slack [flexibility] and I am indebted.
>
> (Hilary)

Hilary received social and emotional capital from her tutor during college hours so this did not impinge on her time with the children or affect her family routines. But it was vital, as she received encouragement from someone who understood the pressures she was under, juggling family life and study. A student who has no family capital needs support from some other source.

When family support is lacking, seek support and encouragement elsewhere. Building a relationship with your tutor and the teaching staff can help you deal with concerns and pinpoint areas where you need further support, be it study skills or encouragement and reassurance, or guidance about financial support and student funding streams. Building friendship groups at college, as Betty did, or accessing old friendship groups, like Jennifer, can also be a way to acquire emotional and possibly cultural support:

> I was making friends again, I'd been so isolated … coming here [university] and making friends and getting my brain engaged it kind of made me feel a little bit like the person I was before.
>
> (Betty)

Students who had no family capital or any acknowledgement and appreciation of their HE studies had the hardest time. Even those who had some access to family capital from their partner craved recognition and support from their parents. Most important to all the women was the potential benefit for their children of their qualification, and trying to minimize the impact of their studies on their children.

As a student, you should be aware that not everyone will share your goals and ambitions. Lacking family capital can be difficult as you want opportunities to share your studies with others and gain emotional and practical support. When this is missing from your family (as for Hilary), it is important to look for other sources such as friends or tutors and staff.

Transformation as a result of support

If you are in a position where you are gaining family capital and support from your partner and family members, you can hope to experience the transformations seen in the shaded boxes of Figure 8.2.

Having time for study affords a transformative space to reflect and reconsider your views and perspectives as well as acquiring new knowledge. As the family adapts to your changing role in the home, you have the chance to transform your identity as a mother and woman. The practical and emotional support you receive makes you feel valued and that your HE studies are accepted.

This chapter has demonstrated that large sources of family capital or investments from partners, children and parents enable students to succeed in HE studies. Such emotional, cultural, economic and social support requires time from others. Within my model of family capital, aspects are not entirely separate and can merge together. In the ideal scenario, practical support with proofreading (cultural capital) and reallocating household and childcare tasks to nurture a shared goal (social capital) often leads to encouragement (which builds a woman's emotional capital). Male partners have the largest capacity for family capital as they have greatest influence on the woman's capacity to study because of the intimacy of their relationship. They are together on a day-to-day basis. This study found that the most instrumental factors in this support were financial, having an educational background so valuing HE studies, and having a strong and supportive relationship. Men who displayed these qualities were willing to invest cultural, economic, social and emotional capital to giving both practical and emotional support. They may face some pressure as they learn new skills to undertake household tasks or childcare. A woman's HE studies can cause stress to the whole family, as Ross, Alan and Bradley relate.

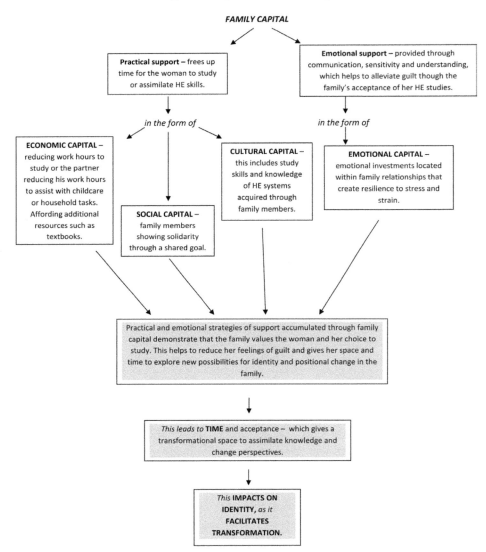

Figure 8.2: Changes that family capital engenders

All the women in the study had prioritized which family members should be least affected by their studying (see Figure 8.3).

PRIORITY 1 – Their children

PRIORITY 2 – Their partner

PRIORITY 3 – Their parents

Figure 8.3: Hierarchy of priority of family members for women students

Children occupied the highest position. The women put many strategies in place to ensure that their children did not lose out because of their studies. To justify what they were doing, they especially needed to demonstrate to others and to themselves that their children were coping and happy. We can see that, for some women, children became providers of family capital as well as consuming it, although it was unexpected.

The women's second priority was their partner. Partners had the potential to give the largest amount of time, of economic capital, of social and emotional capital in the form of solidarity and encouragement, as well as the cultural capital of study support. And their relationship remained important.

Parents were the women's third priority. Receiving family capital from parents built on their childhoods. Parents also assisted with childcare (which helped financially) and fostered their daughter's emotional capital by encouraging and taking pride in their studies. Although having childcare support was important, the women valued the emotional capital in particular. This could be because they usually received childcare from their partners. Their partners also largely shared their career goal so there was already solidarity there. When parents failed to give emotional support for their daughter's studying, the women became resentful.

These findings illustrate the complexity of decision-making and prioritizing within family relationships. Access to large resources of family capital alleviates the guilt of studying. It increases the time women can devote to their HE studies and their motivation. It helps if, even before they begin, the women discuss with their families the possible changes to family routines that result from their studies as this can help forestall potential tensions. Some of the stories told here may help families consider the potential difficulties and what the solutions might be.

Strategies for gaining family support

The following strategies are designed to help you maximize the opportunities to develop support from your family while you are studying:

- Don't be afraid to ask for help from others, whether for IT skills, proofreading or childcare. You do not have to struggle alone.
- Be aware that family members give their time to offer you support and seek ways to show your appreciation.
- Understand the reasons why partners give support (financial, emotional/relational, dependent on academic background) as this may help you to justify your study to your partner.

Strategies for managing to study without support from your family

If you have no family capital when studying while raising children, the following strategies may help:

- Keep in mind why you are doing this programme of study, and the future benefits to you and your family. Remind yourself that the advantages outweigh the disadvantages.
- Try not to feel guilty. Be prepared to be flexible to maximize the support you are offered.
- Not all families will offer capital support; consider where you can access this instead in terms of emotional support, cultural capital support (e.g. study skills) or financial support (e.g. advice). Your university can advise you about guidance on study skills and finance, as will colleagues on the HE programme.
- Draw on the strategies suggested in Chapter 7 for managing your time and overcoming your feelings of guilt.
- Follow Hilary's example: do what works for you. See where your priorities lie, access the support you can, and find ways around barriers, or accept that 'you can only do what you can do'. Being realistic about what is achievable will help you balance family life and HE studies.

These findings will inform prospective women HE students and their tutors about the pressures of their studying on their families. The issues can be raised at admission interviews, induction and between students and their families so that strategies can be put in place to facilitate their studies.

Concluding remarks

This final chapter summarizes this book and considers the implications for women HE students and their families, and for HE institutions.

HE impacts on women's identity and position in the family

Women often view their identity as mothers as the most important aspect of who they are, more important than being a partner, daughter, sibling, friend or worker. When women have taken traditionally gendered roles in the home before they embark on HE, their identity may well be transformed during their studies. Through HE study they develop confidence and self-esteem. This facilitates reflective and analytical thinking and changes their perspectives on life.

The majority of partners and children will adapt to the time constraints caused by the woman studying and many rally round to share household tasks. Family dynamics and routines change. Unlike in earlier decades, my research found most families to be flexible and accommodating.

Effects of HE on women's long-term relationships

Some families go through an initial period of tension and friction but families in which relationships were strong and stable proved to be resilient enough to cope with the additional pressure and strain.

Discussions between the partners can become richer, and mutual respect stronger. The men who are open to their partner's identity change are generally more receptive and accommodating to shifts in home routines and tasks when they see the benefits of transformation.

My study has shown how the women's individual identity transformation can alter the views other people have of them, and others' actions towards them. Previous studies (Biesta *et al.*, 2011; Edwards, 1993a; Merrill, 1999; Parr, 2000; Pascall and Cox, 1993; Schuller *et al.*, 2004) focused on transformations to women students as a result of HE and recognized that this can be positive for their children, but the studies did not consider the effect on the women's partners. My study records that the partners' parenting approaches were transformed, and both parents confirmed this. This challenges Mezirow's theory (1991) of transformation being an insular and self-absorbing experience and recognizes that as the woman's identity changed, families were often transformed.

Children generally adapt well to their mother studying, particularly when she takes care to minimize any negative effects. Women become educational role models for their children and can better support their child's educational development with their increased knowledge about education and its importance. Men tend to spend more time with their children and become more aware of their needs, which enhanced the father's bond with their children. My study shows that families shift, evolve and adapt to changes in the family environment.

Family capital

Family capital is key to providing support for women students and aiding their transformation. Women who have access to large resources of family capital readily develop cultural awareness and the skills of HE as they devote time to their HE studies.

Factors in family capital include building the emotional capital of encouragement and support, growing one's cultural capital in understanding the HE environment, having the economic capital to invest in resources, as well as the social capital of solidarity. When women embark on HE studies, their partners are usually the main providers of family capital. Men afford these students family capital because they also value education. If their relationship is strong, they will want to be supportive.

Women whose partners offer no support for their studies can seek educational support from other family members, friends or staff at their HE institution. Possibly, the couple may try to work through the barriers HE studies are seen to cause.

Families that offer capital for the mother to study are also more receptive to change and more accepting of the women's personal transformation and the changes to family roles and parenting techniques.

A key message of this book for students and prospective students is that HE has the potential to change you as a person, change your role within the family, modify family routines and ultimately relationships between immediate and wider family members, as the women's stories show. I hope readers have drawn upon these stories to reflect on their own experience and make sense of it. As the students have testified, it is worth the effort personally, professionally and for the family as a whole:

> Never in my wildest dreams, did I think I would be able to go to university. I knew I was capable of something, but university was just over my head ... I just thought university was all beyond me ... Becoming a mature student is not an easy option; it's a big

commitment. But for me I took the plunge, there was a part of me that found it satisfying, wondering why I didn't do it earlier. My proudest moment was when I went on to win the 'student of the year' award, I may not have been the most academic student in the group, but I was not going to quit, 'quitters don't make winners' was the quote that kept me going.

(Esme)

Suggestions for lecturers and policymakers

This study has used empirical research to demonstrate that HE study is transformative to women students' lives, and to outline how lack of family capital can make studying problematic. The research will help HE staff to highlight the possible transformative effects of HE study on family life for potential women students and their partners, and stress how important it is for the family to invest large resources of family capital into making HE easier for the women students. The women in families who nonetheless have no access to family capital will benefit from a network of emotional and social support from university staff and peers. Tutors should be aware of the complexities faced by mothers who are studying and promote peer group and study skills support, as well as helping women to develop strategies for finding study time.

Women who, like Hilary, cannot access family capital may require opportunities to develop emotional capital so as to build confidence and self-belief; and also study skills support to enhance their cultural capital, and opportunities to network and build peer relationships to develop social capital. Therefore policymakers need to be aware of the importance of timetabling teaching so that students are given the time and opportunity to develop the personal resources to juggle HE studies and family life.

Marie's remarks

Marie's remarks are a fitting end to this book:

Returning to higher education as a mature student has been the most challenging, demanding, brilliant and ultimately life-changing experience. Admittedly, after over two decades without any sort of formal studying, the first days of my course could be likened to being in a washing machine or being thrown in at the deep end of a pool with a wave machine on full power. However, staying afloat is definitely worth it.

Socially it can be a daunting experience even for those with good personal skills and confidence. Younger students may have the upper hand when it comes to getting going academically, being Internet savvy or connecting to one another on social media; but remember you can bring maturity and experience into your work, so use what you have to your advantage. Think long term, plan well, stay focused and forgive yourself when things don't go to plan, and remember to be flexible and allow your goals to evolve.

Treat the children to your time and attention when the pressure is off and let them celebrate your successes too. Try not to worry too much about the feelings of guilt when assignments are due and the children feel like they are second place; my son has a lot of Lego as a result of my degree. Rest assured the pride and exhilaration you will feel when they tell you how proud they are and that you are an inspiration to them far surpasses the negative feelings, for both them and you. Finally, learn to trust in someone on your course if you can; friendship comes when you least expect it and in the least obvious places but sharing the journey makes it so much more fulfilling.

There will be highs and there will be lows. However, whether you are looking for a new career, new experiences, new direction, or just to do something that is not what the people around you expect you to do, the journey is empowering. It has given me the strength to stand up for what I believe in and have pride in myself as an individual and it has given me back my self-respect. In addition, I have been able to show my children that it is never too late to chase a dream or goal, even if they think forty-something is ancient!

References

Biesta, G.J.J., Field, J., Hodkinson, P., Macleod, F.J. and Goodson, I.F. (2011) *Improving Learning through the Lifecourse: Learning lives.* Oxon: Routledge.

Bourdieu, P. (1986) 'The forms of capital'. In Szeman, I. and Kaposy, T. (eds; 2011) *Cultural Theory: An anthology.* Oxford: Wiley-Blackwell, 81–93.

— (1991) *Language and Symbolic Power.* Cambridge: Polity Press.

Bowl, M. (2003) *Non-Traditional Entrants to Higher Education: 'They talk about people like me'.* Staffordshire: Trentham Books.

Brooks, R. (2015) 'Social and spatial disparities in emotional responses to education: Feelings of "guilt" among student-parents'. *British Educational Research Journal,* 41 (3), 505–19.

Burke, P.J. and Jackson, S. (2007) *Reconceptualising Lifelong Learning: Feminist interventions.* Abingdon: Routledge.

Burr, V. (2003) *Social Constructionism.* 2nd ed. Hove: Routledge.

Cherrington, S. and Thornton, K. (2013) 'Continuing professional development in early childhood education in New Zealand'. *Early Years,* 33 (2), 119–32.

Christie, H., Tett, L., Cree, V.E., Hounsell, J. and McCune, V. (2008) 'A real rollercoaster of confidence and emotions: Learning to be a university student'. *Studies in Higher Education,* 33 (5), 567–81.

Coleman, J.S. (1988) 'Social capital in the creation of human capital'. *American Journal of Sociology,* 94, 95–120.

Davies, B. and Harré, R. (1999) 'Positioning and personhood'. In Harré, R. and van Langenhove, L. (eds) *Positioning Theory.* Oxford: Blackwell Publishers, 32–52.

Davies, P., Qiu, T. and Davies, M. (2014) 'Cultural and human capital, information and higher education choices'. *Journal of Education Policy,* 29 (6), 804–25.

Department for Education (DfE) (2013) *More great childcare. Raising quality and giving parents more choice.* Online. www.gov.uk/government/uploads/system/uploads/attachment_data/file/170552/More_20Great_20Childcare_20v2.pdf (accessed 28 February 2017).

Doucet, A. (2006) *Do Men Mother? Fathering, care and domestic responsibility.* Toronto: University of Toronto Press.

Edwards, R. (1993a) *Mature Women Students: Separating or connecting family and education.* Taylor and Francis: London.

Edwards, R. (1993b) 'Shifting status: Mothers' higher education and their children's schooling'. In David, M., Edwards, R., Hughes, M. and Ribbens, J. (eds) *Mothers and Education: Inside out? Exploring family-education policy and experience.* Basingstoke: Macmillan Press Ltd, 181–284.

Equality and Human Rights Commission (EHRC) (2009) *Working Better: Fathers, family and work – contemporary perspectives.* Research summary 41. EHRC. Online. www.equalityhumanrights.com/sites/default/files/research-summary-41-working-better-fathers-family-and-work_0.pdf (accessed 28 February 2017).

Erichsen, E.A. (2011) 'Learning for change: Transforming international experience as identity work'. *Journal of Transformative Education,* 9 (2), 109–33.

Etherington, K. (2004) *Becoming a Reflexive Researcher*. London: Jessica Kingsley Publishers.

Fatherhood Institute (2016) *2016 Fairness in Families Index, Capstone Project*. Online. www.fatherhoodinstitute.org/wp-content/uploads/2016/06/ FINALFatherhood-Institute-Capstone-FiFI-2016.pdf (accessed 28 February 2017).

Feenay, B.C. and Lemay, E.P. (2012) 'Surviving relationship threats: The role of emotional capital'. *Personality and Social Psychology Bulletin*, 38 (8), 1004–17.

Gofen, A. (2009) 'Family capital: How first-generation higher education students break the intergenerational cycle'. *Family Relations*, 58, 104–20.

Green Lister, P. (2003) 'It's like you can't be a whole person, a mother who studies. Lifelong learning: Mature women students with caring commitments in social work education'. *Social Work Education: The International Journal*, 22 (2), 125–38.

Griffiths, V. (2002) 'Crossing boundaries: The experiences of mature student mothers in initial teacher education'. *International Journal of Inclusive Education*, 6 (3), 267–85.

Harré, R. and van Lagenhove, L. (1999) 'The dynamics of social episodes'. In Harré, R. and van Langenhove, L. (eds) *Positioning Theory*. Oxford: Blackwell Publishers, 1–13.

Heenan, D. (2002) 'Women, access and progression: An examination of women's reasons for not continuing in higher education following the completion of the Certificate in Women's Studies'. *Studies in Continuing Education*, 24 (1), 39–55.

Hughes, C. (2002) *Women's Contemporary Lives: In and beyond the mirror*. London: Routledge.

Jamieson, A., Sabates, R., Woodley, A. and Feinstein, L. (2009) 'The benefits of higher education study for part-time students'. *Studies in Higher Education*, 34 (3), 245–62.

Jenkins, R. (2002) *Pierre Bourdieu*. Oxon: Routledge.

— (2008) *Social Identity*. 3rd ed. Abingdon: Routledge.

Lawler, S. (2000) *Mothering the Self. Mothers, daughters, subjects*. Routledge: London.

Lehrer, J.S. (2013) 'Accompanying early childhood professional reflection in Quebec: A case study'. *Early Years*, 33 (7), 186–200.

McFall, S.L. (ed.) (2012) *Understanding Society: Findings 2012*. Colchester: Institute for Social and Economic Research, University of Essex.

Marandet, E. and Wainwright, E. (2010) 'Invisible experiences: Understanding the choices and needs of university students with dependent children'. *British Educational Research Journal*, 36 (5), 787–805.

Mercer, J. (2007) 'The challenges of insider research in educational institutions: Wielding a double edged sword and resolving delicate dilemmas'. *Oxford Review of Education*, 33 (1), 1–17.

Merrill, B. (1999) *Gender, Change and Identity: Mature women students in university*. Aldershot: Ashgate.

Mezirow, J. (1978) 'Perspective transformation'. *Adult Education Quarterly*, 28 (10), 100–10.

Mezirow, J. (1991) *Transformative Dimensions of Adult Learning*. California: Jossey-Bass Inc.

Mezirow, J. (2000) *Learning as Transformation: Critical perspectives on a theory in progress*. San Francisco: Jossey-Bass.

Morgan, J. (2011) *Rethinking Family Practices*. London: Palgrave Macmillan.

Oakley, A. (ed.) (2005) *The Ann Oakley Reader: Gender, women and social science*. Bristol: Policy Press.

Office for National Statistics (ONS) (2013) *Education and training statistics for the UK: 2013*. Online. www.gov.uk/government/statistics/education-and-training-statistics-for-the-uk-2013 (accessed 28 February 2017).

Osgood, J. (2006) 'Professionalism and performativity: The feminist challenge over-simplification of mature learners' experience(s)'. *Research in Post-Compulsory Education*, 26 (2), 187–99.

Parr, J. (2000) *Identity and Education: The links for mature women students*. Aldershot: Ashgate.

Parsons, T. (1959) *The Social System*. New York: The Free Press.

Pascall, G. and Cox, R. (1993) *Women Returning to Higher Education*. SRHE: Buckingham.

Plageman, P.M. and Sabina, C. (2010) 'Perceived family influence on undergraduate adult female students'. *The Journal of Continuing Higher Education*, 58, 156–66.

Putnam, R. (2000) *Bowling Alone: The collapse and revival of American community*. New York: Simon and Schuster Paperbacks.

Reay, D. (2003) 'A risky business? Mature working-class women students and access to higher education correspondence'. *Gender and Education*, 15 (3), 301–17.

— (2004) 'Gendering Bourdieu's concepts of capitals? Emotional capital, women and social class'. *The Sociological Review*, 48 (4), 568–85.

Reynolds, T., Callender, C. and Edwards, R. (2003) *Caring and Counting: The impact of mothers' employment on family relationships*. Bristol: Policy Press.

Schuller, T., Preston, J., Hammond, C., Brassett-Grundy, A. and Bynner, J. (2004) *The Benefits of Learning: The impact of education on health, family life and social capital*. London: Routledge Falmer.

Scott, J. (2014) *Oxford Dictionary of Sociology*. 4th ed. Oxford: Oxford University Press.

Snape, D. and Finch, S. (2006) *Evaluation of the Early Years Sector-Endorsed Foundation Degree: Report of the follow-up student survey*. London: Department for Education and Skills.

Taylor, G. and Spencer, S. (2004) *Social Identities: Multidisciplinary approach*. London: Routledge.

Thompson, S. and Thompson, N. (2008) *The Critically Reflective Practitioner*. Basingstoke: Palgrave Macmillan.

Walkerdine, V. (2006) 'Workers in the new economy: Transformation as border crossing'. *Ethos,* 34 (1), 89–122.

Webb, J., Schirato, T. and Danaher, D. (2002) *Understanding Bourdieu*. London: Sage Publications.

Webber, L. (2014) 'Accessing HE for non-traditional students: "Outside of my position"'. *Research in Post Compulsory Education*, 19 (1), 91–106.

Williams, F. (2004) *Rethinking Families*. London: Calouste Gulbenkian Foundation.

References

Winkle-Wagner, R. (2010) *Cultural Capital: The promises and pitfalls in educational research*. United States: Wiley Subscription Services.

Young, M. and Wilmott, P. (1973) *The Symmetrical Family*. Middlesex: Penguin Books.

Zembylas, M. (2007) 'Emotional capital and education: Theoretical insights from Bourdieu'. *British Journal of Educational Studies*, 55 (4), 443–63.

Index

Index